Real Men

Initial Steps to Male Significance

Tim Mays

Copyright © 2012 Author Name

All rights reserved.

ISBN: 1984220950
ISBN-13: 9781984220950

DEDICATION

I dedicate this book to fathers.

First, to my earthly father, Harry B. Mays, who taught me "that a good name is to be chosen rather than riches, loving favor rather than silver and gold." He showed me how to love the wife of my youth and stay committed to her until death separates you. He did the best that he knew how to provide me opportunities that I now recognize have not been afforded to all men.

Next, to the men God placed in my life to fill the voids of my earthly father.

Then, to men who are making every effort to be a good father even though they may not know exactly what it looks like.

Finally, to the men who have seen the need to father the fatherless and stepped up as mentors to make an impact in the lives of men.

CONTENTS

Acknowledgments

Introduction 1

Step 1 - Acknowledge the Problem 12

Step 2 – Understand You Have Issues and Decide to Overcome Them 24

Step 3 – Seek Forgiveness for Yourself and Then Forgive Others 46

Step 4 – Understand and Pursue Healthy Relationships 61

Step 5 – Understand That Evil Exists and Must Be Battled Daily 93

Be Somebody and Do Something 98

Final Thoughts 109

Notes 116

Tim Mays

ACKNOWLEDGMENTS

First and foremost, I want to thank my Lord and Savior Jesus Christ for saving me in 1983. Then, He gave me the abilities and opportunities to get to this point in my life and did not give up on me. He has been patient with me as I "become."

Next, I want thank my wife Jill for being my partner in this journey called life. I am blessed to have such a beautiful person, inside and out, to be the wind beneath my wings. You have encouraged me and not given up when I have failed to love and lead well. You are my compliment and I would not be who I am without you by my side. I love you with all that I am and all that I have!

I am grateful for all who were willing to share your heart and life's journey to help others.

Brother Larry Eugene Lother, you have been such an inspiration and encouragement to me. Your insistence that I write this book has kept me on task. I can't wait to see how God uses this material. I value your friendship and you have played a big part in my spiritual growth in becoming. Thank you for helping with the content revisions.

To my friend and brother, Mark Bagwell, who agreed to be the guarder of my soul by being honest with me and provided a safe place to be vulnerable. You have helped me understand that I am loved and favored by my Heavenly Father. Thank you for helping shape the content of the book as well.

Chandler, my beloved son in who I am well pleased, thank you for the cover design and artwork. I am so honored to be your Dad.

To Bo Metcalfe for correcting and sourcing the material in the book.

And finally, to Tony Moore for helping get this project across the finish line.

INTRODUCTION

That which has been is what will be, that which is done will be done, and there is nothing new under the sun. Ecclesiastes 1:9 NKJV

Life is a process; a journey, and not a destination. Through books I have read, godly people in my life, and messages from different ministers, God has been working in my life to show me what He created me for. Recently, I have been challenged and led to move forward in sharing with men what He has taught me in my masculine journey to this point. This book is a continuation of finally listening to my heavenly Father and making a difference for His kingdom on earth. Solomon told us, *There is nothing new under the sun,* so most of the content in this book is what I have learned from others. My goal is to share the application of the information in my life and the lives of other men who I have had the pleasure and honor to journey. I also want the book to be a resource for you to get information and guidance for yourself. You were born on purpose, for a purpose, and with a purpose. My prayer is that the material in this book will help in your journey to find it.

This part of my journey started when my wife's coworker suggested that I read a book that had really impacted his life and his masculine journey. I purchased *Wild at Heart* by John Eldredge and started reading. Emotions and struggles I knew were there but had been unable to verbalize suddenly were revealed to me. Though I knew I had missed something in my relationship with my daddy, I never understood the impact it had on my life and the decisions I have made. My friend and mentoring inspiration, Regi Campbell, said it well, "When you are lost, the first thing you have to do is figure out where you are."[1] A majority of the masculine battle is to understand the dynamics of the situation and where you are in the process. I was motivated to dig deeper and get "un-lost" in my journey. I had great influences in my life and had been following Christ for more than twenty years, serving in different areas. I had a family, and by the grace of God, the ministry of Focus on the Family, Promise Keepers and other organizations, I understood what being a good husband and father looked like. I was even making a respectable effort at applying the principles. But this book rocked my world! I found what was missing, and I wanted to fill it with the things of God and not man. Like a Lays

1

potato chip, you can't just read the book once and be satisfied, so I read it over again with other Eldredge books – I was addicted.

My oldest daughter, Abby, had a young man introduced into her life through one of her classmates at the Medical University of South Carolina as she pursued her physical therapist degree. He was a bright young man who had decided that the military was a better option for his future than college, where he was having a good time at the expense of his academic pursuits. Soon after we met him, he was deployed to Iraq as a medic in his unit. Sensing that this guy might be around a while, I gave him a copy of the *Wild at Heart* book to read in his spare time, which he would have plenty of where he was going. The power of the information was affirmed when I received a text from him stating, "I just finished the book and have never felt this way about myself as a man and my relationship with God. I don't know how to thank you other than be the man Abby deserves." I have asked my son-in-law, Alex, to share his story with you and what understanding masculine strength has done and is doing for him.

* * * *

My name is Alex, and on October 17, 2010, I found Christ. This is the story of my life and my journey to a relationship with Christ.

I grew up in a "Christian" home and had always been close to and affiliated with organized Protestant churches. I grew up with the notion that church was associated with following the rules to get to heaven. I dressed up in my Sunday best, sang hymns and said the Lord's Prayer without thinking about the meaning of it all. Although I faithfully attended church on Sundays and Wednesdays, I never felt a real connection with Christ, nor did I truly understand what it meant to have a relationship with Him. Church was much like everything else in my life at the time; just another obligation that my parents subjected me to.

I was born into a hostile household with an unemployed, alcoholic, drug-using father and a mother attempting to fulfill the role of both parents, while trying to provide for my siblings and me. As a result, my parents divorced before my first birthday. My mother remarried a man that she knew from her time in the Navy. She settled with my step-father because she was desperate for a positive male figure in our lives and thought he might fit the bill. My stepdad, however, was ill-prepared for the tribulations that accompany fatherhood in a blended family. Coupled with my mother's overcompensation from a lifetime of being let down by every man in her life, and a firm impenetrable wall she constructed around herself and her children, my stepdad didn't stand a chance. Childhood for me was a long and seemingly endless road of arguing, strife, and hostility.

My biological father moved a great distance away and secluded himself to a fringe-like existence on open land far from any discernable resemblance of a normal society. Early in my childhood, he made a genuine attempt at fatherhood; however, as the years passed, he became less and less concerned with the need to hide anything from us. He began drinking heavily, even during our scheduled visits. Eventually, after his second wife left him, he stopped caring at all. I would wake up at nine o'clock in the morning and he would already be on the verge of passing out with empty beer cans piling up in the front yard. My older sister eventually stopped going to my father's house altogether because of his drinking. My father's drinking was a hard pill to swallow, but was nothing compared to the subsequent repercussions of an alcoholic existence on loved ones. To this day, at least 75 percent of the phone calls I receive from my father are with him in a drunken state. Throughout childhood, and even today, my father has constantly made promises and broken them. His drinking has made it impossible for any kind of "normal" father/son relationship, despite my efforts and desires. He continues to live by himself in the middle of nowhere, making the same promises he never intends to keep, drifting further from society, and Christ, with every bottle of alcohol he buys.

After graduating high school, I went to college and tried to find myself again. I managed to drink away 2 years and $45,000 in student loans before I realized I needed to make a change. After leaving college, I returned home to my mother's house to make some tough decisions. I realized that life was catching up with me quickly, and I wasn't prepared. Fearful of never amounting to anything, and student loans breathing down my neck, I made the decision to join the Army. Within three months of being home, I enlisted in the Army and left for basic training.

The military lifestyle came easy to me. Growing up in a

militarily structured home, I was used to immense stress on a daily basis. I was placed in leadership positions throughout all phases of my training, and I began to excel above my expectations, proving that I had what it took. After training, I reported to the 1st Infantry Division, where I was assigned as the Senior Line Medic for an Infantry Company. I continued to excel and progress in my military career. I took great pride in the fact that when my senior leadership needed something done, I was the one they called upon. Throughout this time, I matured greatly and realized, for the first time, that I had value and purpose in my life; but, something was still missing. Even though my career was developing above my expectations and everything in my life seemed to be falling into place, I still didn't feel content.

Not long after arriving to my unit, I took a trip home to visit my older sister for a long weekend. During my visit, I met a young woman, Abby, who would eventually become my wife. I had no idea that this chance meeting was a crucial turning point in my life.

Abby's childhood was the polar opposite of mine. She grew up in a stable, faith-based household, where love and respect flourished. Her parents were still married and she had beautiful relationships with every member of her family. Her parents instilled the importance of a relationship with God, as opposed to religious institutions. I was immediately drawn to her, and we cultivated a strong relationship, despite being 1400 miles away from each other. Eventually, the time came to meet her parents. Feeling so strongly for Abby, I was more than eager to do so, but I could not help fearing that I wasn't good enough for someone like her and that her parents would know it all the same. This was not the case. In fact, it was an event that further changed my life forever. During our very first meeting, Abby's father showed me something that I had never seen before; what a father looks like. I was humbled by the way he treated his family and how deep the bonds between them were. THIS was what I wanted for myself. This was what I'd been looking for. This was what I never knew I didn't have. On that day, Tim Mays became my hero. Over the weeks and months to come, Tim and I remained in frequent contact with each other. I enjoyed speaking with him and having an older male in my life to talk with when I had something nagging at the back of my mind. But still, something seemed to be missing.

About ten months into my relationship with Abby, I received

news that once again altered the course of my life. I was being reassigned to a Brigade Combat Team deploying to Iraq within two months. Before I left for Iraq, Tim sent me a gift. It was a copy of John Eldredge's *Wild at Heart*, with an inscription that read, "This book changed my life; I wish I would have read it when I was a younger man." Although I appreciated the thought, I wasn't what you would call a big reader at the time. But nevertheless, I thanked him and left for Iraq.

My unit originally stopped in Kuwait for a period to train and acclimate to the harsh environment. Having ample downtime, I decided to take a look at the book Tim gave me. I didn't have a great deal of motivation at first, so the first bit took me a couple of days. As I read the words on these seemingly harmless pages, my heart and soul were slowly released from the chains of my life. My eyes were forced open to the emotional travesties of my life, and for the first time, I was able to see how the past events of my life affected my present and future. But most importantly, I finally realized what I had been missing all along; A real relationship with God. Not an "oh-no, someone help me relationship." Not an "I want to go to heaven so I better be good relationship." A real relationship with God.

Sitting in a tent in Kuwait, reading words I had heard thousands of times but never knew the meaning, I made the decision to surrender myself and my life to Christ. I still remember every sensation I felt that night; the sounds, the smells, the emotions, are forever burned in my mind. I realized that I had deeply seeded wounds that could only be healed through a relationship with Christ. In that moment I prayed, "Lord God I surrender myself to you. All that I am now and forever will be for You. Please come into my heart and heal the wounds of my wickedness and show me how it is to be a disciple of your word." A wave of fulfilling relief swept over me like a bright warm light at the break of a new day. I felt God's embrace throughout my whole body. As quickly and suddenly as it had started, I heard a faint voice say, "It's okay, Alex I've been waiting here for you."

At first, I was blind, but now I see. It took traveling halfway across the world to a distant warzone to realize that all of the events of my life happened to bring me to a point where I was ready for a relationship with Christ. I had to fail out of college to join the Army. I had to have a difficult childhood to excel in the

Army. I had to excel in the Army to realize my worth and mature into a man. I had to mature into a young man to be ready for a relationship with a woman like Abby. I had to have a tumultuous relationship with my father in order to appreciate and yearn for that in a relationship with my father-in-law, Tim. And finally, I had to deploy to Iraq to realize that there was a hole in my heart that only Jesus could fill.

I never felt so alive. I finished the book in two days and was now facing a new-found knowledge of the contributing facts of my life, but no real source of experience to draw from to work through my wounds. I began communicating with Tim and chaplains of my unit to talk about the struggles I was facing and to further my relationship with God. Additionally, I started a small group of fellowship with some of the members of my unit to talk about a lot of the issues that we deal with on professional and personal levels. Through the fellowship with these men, and a relationship with the first true father figure in my life, I was able to move mountains in my spiritual life. I realized that it wasn't enough to just identify the scars of my past, but that I had to do something about them. The first and hardest step would be to settle my relationship with my father. I had carried years of disappointment and hatred towards him, for the grievances of my youth. It was tearing me apart, and I didn't recognize it. I came to the realization that most of the transgressions of my father were a result of shortcomings of his own father. I realized that I could not move forward in my relationship with Christ until I mended my relationship with my earthly father. From Iraq, I decided to call him and forgive him for everything that had transpired between us in my life. I expected him to breakdown and come to the realization that I was right, and that he had been abusing our relationship for years, and that he was so sorry and everything would be different from here on out. Nope. When I called him, he laughed at me. He refused to acknowledge that there were any wrongs committed on his part, and made me feel like an idiot. Nevertheless, I felt a world of relief to have that weight off my shoulders and that I was able to move forward in my spiritual progress. I continued along my journey for the rest of the deployment, strengthening my relationship with Christ, however, there was something still missing.

When I returned home, Abby and I got married. For the first time in my adult life I went back to church because I wanted to, not because I felt I had to. Even though I had been baptized as a toddler, I got baptized in Christ for the first time and was lucky enough to have my new Father-In-Law, Tim, be the one who baptized me. My beautiful wife, Abby, convinced me that I was capable of more than I thought and inspired me to apply to a Physician Assistant Program through the Army that I was accepted into. Now that my relationship with Christ, not my circumstances, guides me through life, I am able to live for Him and without the chains of humanity dragging me from prosperity. Everything that has happened to me in my life has been preparing me for a task for which God placed me on this earth. I may not completely understand what that is right now, but I am being prepared for it spiritually every day. Both the pain and the beauty in my life made me the man I am today, a child of God.

* * * *

The next "aha moment" was in a message at my church, when my pastor made the statement, "When you discover your misery, you will discover your ministry." Misery is what breaks your heart and also breaks God's heart. In other words, what makes you think "somebody needs to do something about that!"? For me, God had been stirring in my heart that we have a father crisis in this country, and it is because men have abandoned their divinely-appointed role in the family, the church and the community – somebody does need to do something! What I saw was:

1. Men who are struggling to find purpose, but fearful to reach out for help. Meanwhile, men are creating chaos in society as they look for purpose in the wrong places
2. A society treating the symptoms of a problem, unaware of the source or unwilling to call a spade a damn shovel in order to deal with it
3. A secularized and feminized definition of manhood
4. A general male crisis
5. An overwhelming mess that we have let ourselves get into

God has not called us to make excuses, but rather to make a

difference. We need godly men to mentor other males and make a difference by showing them what a godly man looks like. I realized that I had spent my life trying to be successful and not significant. Significance is making a difference in the lives of others and making the world a better place while bringing the glory to God. Realizing that I had lived over half of my life, I wanted to finish well. God has made an investment in me and expects me to use what He gave me. That is what we will all give account for and He will not accept excuses. It was time for me to really make a difference, and I now know some things that can help others along their journey. It is an overwhelming task at this point, but like the little boy throwing starfish back in the ocean, I can make a difference for "that one." I just need to keep my eyes open and seize each moment that I am given. I now had what Bill Hybels calls, "holy discontent."

I have been a huge follower of Tony Dungy, reading everything he has published. In his book, *The Mentor Leader*, he states my purpose so appropriately,

> Judges who review presentencing investigative reports will tell you that the absence of a father or a positive male figure is a key indicator in the lives of the people they sentence to time in prison. We need strong men to build into the lives of our younger men and boys. Not extraordinary people; just ordinary, everyday men who care enough to invest themselves – their time, attention, and wisdom – in the lives of others, whether as part of their natural leadership environment or as an additional relationship they purposefully undertake.[2]

Now, the question was "how do I get men to understand this and engage?"

A Google search of Christian mentoring led me to a book called *Mentoring Like Jesus* by Regi Campbell. After reading it and exploring his website, radicalmentoring.com, I was on my way!

Seeing first-hand the power of the *Wild at Heart* material in my life and Alex's, I purchased the training material and recruited a group of guys to go through it, expecting the fire to be lit under them as well. The sessions go for several weeks and are most effective in a group that has an on-going commitment such as church training, home groups, or other regular gatherings. The men were sporadic in attending weekly, but I saw the need and power of the material to change a man's life. I also saw that men will do something if they feel enabled and there is a short-term time commitment. So I set out to develop a four or five week training with the main content of *Wild at Heart* along with additional material to motivate a man to mentor other males so that they gain a better understanding of what a godly man should look like.

I began developing a short-term training that I felt would give guys a boost to move. During the development of the material I have been honored and humbled by the realization that God has asked me to do this for Him then empowered and directed me to do it. As I reviewed materials and began to write it down, the words came, and the thoughts flowed onto the paper. I look back at what was written and think, "Did I write that?" I did, but only with the help of the Holy Spirit has any of it been possible. Out of this, the *Manhood* curriculum was born. Most of this book will come from its content, and you will see that I had help.

Still stirred by the misery God put in my heart, I was seeking what it would look like to get men enabled and motivated to mentor other males. I meet with a great group of guys on Wednesday mornings where we take turns sharing what God is teaching us in our lives. The leader for the day is responsible not only for the material, but the biscuits too! On one particular day, our local FCA director, Mac, was sharing, using Nehemiah as his text. When Nehemiah saw the situation and the disgrace of Jerusalem, he knew it was time to rebuild the wall. While I have never heard the audible voice of God, I have learned what it sounds like in my heart, and I heard Him loud and clear say, "you need to rebuild real men. Men who understand the strength that I gave them and what I put them here for – to lead My way!" I left that morning with the name of what God had given me to do, *ReBuild Real Men*.

We wanted this to have an appeal to men, not in a church way, but something "manly" as the logo to promote what we do. I saw it in an advertisement and immediately knew, DeWalt can be converted to ReBuild. A local business, Diamond T Promotions, has been very supportive of what I am doing, and my good friend Tyler created the logo and we were set to go. Our vision is Generational Manhood with the mission to impact men to discover who they are in Christ, then empower and facilitate their investment into other men and boys – one life at a time.

Initially four men went through the *Manhood* class, providing feedback for improvements. At the same time, I began approaching people that I trust to guide me in creating a training module for male mentors. The *Manhood* material took on a life of its own and has been presented to numerous groups on an ongoing basis. Our core team began meeting regularly to discuss how to form the class and get the material they need. Again, I picked books that had really impacted my understanding of what a godly man should embody and pass on to others. The ReBuild Leadership material was developed to provide a well-rounded picture of the tools needed to successfully mentor other males with several classes going through it, but there has been no real sustained interest to seize the many opportunities to make a difference. Therefore, I am spending my time introducing the Radical Mentoring model to churches and planning to recruit the graduates to help implement the vision. Mentoring is not a science but an art because it is people-focused and not program-focused. There is no right or wrong way, just some better ways. It is simply an older guy, at least two seasons ahead according to Regi Campbell [3], sharing what he has learned living life. Men need to feel enabled to share their life's lessons and the venue to put it into practice. That is what ReBuild Real Men is all about.

With all that being said, here we go! Understand that this is not politically correct information. It is biblically correct information. Some have said that it is in your face, but I have found that this is what most men respond to best in order to get it. Albert Einstein said that, "insanity is doing the same thing over and over again and expecting different results." We have tried it the other way and now it is time to go back to God's way. It is time for somebody to do something, and we can't keep doing it the same way. My hope is that you will realize that you can be somebody and do something.

The song I associate with ReBuild Real Men is *Do Something* by Matthew West. We see things wrong in our world and ask God, "why don't You do something about that?" His response is "I did, yeah, I created you!"[4]

What is "it" that God has created you for? Be somebody, do something!

Real Men

The following is information that helped me understand what a "Real Man" looks like. I have broken it down to five steps a man needs to take to get his "Man Card."

STEP 1 – ACKNOWLEDGE THE PROBLEM

Masculine Strength and its designed purpose

When a man functions as designed "...there will be order, authority and provision. Yet when he doesn't, he opens himself up and those connected to him, to a life of chaos."
~ Tony Evans

Houston we have a problem!

Few informed people would disagree that the American male is in trouble. The wave has come ashore and we now see the effects of boys growing up "fatherless." Their fathers are either not physically present in their life, or they are emotionally absent causing the boy feel "on his own" to deal with life in general or in certain areas. Boys who grow up in homes without fathers have more issues that not only affect them but society in general. We see:

- Higher incarceration rates
- Higher instances of behavioral disorders
- Higher high school dropout rates
- Lower educational attainment rates
- Confused identities
- More aggressive behavior
- Lower achievement
- Higher delinquency
- Higher juvenile detention rates
- Higher criminal activity[1]

The importance of developing a legacy of men has been abandoned by our society. We have government assistance programs that actually discourage the traditional family unit. Due to "the man in the house" provision of welfare it is financially advantageous for the male to not be in the house so the home and family suffer. In too many situations the father is physically there but never taught how to be a man by his father as he grew up. The dysfunctional parents have children and the cycle replicates unless outside forces intervene.

This tragedy of father absence is seen in the news when little boys are exploited by men as they seek male connection in their lives. One high profile case that captured the headlines for some time was the Jerry Sandusky situation at Penn State University. In his article for the Philadelphia Inquirer, Ronnie Polaneczky asked the question, "What if so many of Jerry Sandusky's victims hadn't needed father figures in the first place? Easy answer: This never would've happened. He further stated that, of Sandusky's eight known victims (two more remain unidentified), six had no father in their lives and three admitted to never having known their dads at all." The travesty was further cited with the following quotes: "On the witness stand, many boys said they regarded Sandusky as the father they'd never had. He treated me like a son in front of other people...Outside of that, he treated me like his girlfriend," said one victim. Another victim testified, "I didn't want to lose the good things I had. I looked at Jerry as kind of a father figure...I didn't want to lose somebody actually paying attention to me." Polaneczky observed that "Even a child from a wealthy, two-parent home can become a victim if he is emotionally detached from his parents. Or if he has emotional issues that make him vulnerable."[2] Boys are in desperate need of father figures. They will find one or one will find them. This situation has to be addressed, and more laws and money are not the answer.

I was privileged to hear the director of mission control during the Apollo 13 historic mission, Gene Kranz, speak at a conference I attended. He shared the following information that I think is applicable as we address this critical issue in our society.

Foundations of Mission Control

- ✓ To instill within ourselves these qualities essential for professional excellence
  - Discipline
  - Competence
  - Confidence
  - Responsibility
  - Toughness
  - Teamwork

✓ To always be aware that suddenly and unexpectedly we may find ourselves in a role where our performance has ultimate consequences.

✓ To recognize that the greatest error is not to have tried and failed, but that in trying, we did not give our best effort.

"Failure is not an option!"
Gene Kranz, Flight Director Apollo 13

When it comes to restoring biblical masculinity in America, "failure is not an option." I have summarized the approach used in returning our astronauts to earth from the failed mission as a model to pursue restoration of males.

1. Recognized there was a problem
2. Assessed the situation and options for success
3. Worked with other men to determine a plan
4. Implemented the steps
5. Asked God to put His super with their natural for a supernatural outcome

NASA Director: "This could be the worst disaster NASA's ever faced."
Gene Kranz: "With all due respect, sir, I believe this is gonna be our finest hour."

This indeed could be our finest hour if we will unify our effort to rebuilding real men.

Snakes and Snails and Puppy Dog Tails; Sugar and Spice and Everything Nice

Boys and girls are different. There are groups attempting to neuter the American society, trying to convince us that there is no difference in males and females. However, the design is there and cannot be denied by anyone not blinded by an ideology that says otherwise. If one does not believe that boys are different, they have never spent any time with one. Eldredge states it this way, "capes and swords, camouflage, bandanas and six-shooters – these are the uniforms of boyhood. Little boys yearn to know they are powerful, they are dangerous, they are someone to be reckoned with."[3]

Young lives are lived in the story book tale of "Happily Ever After" with the desire for the story extending into adulthood. We pursue the dream of the perfect world and our part in it. Every male wants to be the hero in the story, and the female wants to be the beauty. Good prevails over evil and the boy is the one who makes it happen. Disney has made a fortune telling this story with different characters in a diverse settings but the same theme. Little boys need to hear, "You are a man. You have what it takes!" Little girls need to hear, "You are beautiful and I will fight for you!" Both must hear it from their daddy or a male role model in their lives. If not, they will look to have it answered in many other ways, and none good. They have a broken heart, a wound, which yearns to be healed. This "father wound" is the source of most of our societal issues we are now experiencing. Once I grasped this concept, understanding why people are the way they are becomes clearer as does "The Answer."

The Lion, Man and Jesus

"It is a bad time to be a boy in America. Our culture has turned against the masculine essence, aiming to cut it off early."
~ John Eldredge

Because he is dangerous, the lion is put in a cage for the protection and pleasure of others. A caged lion will eventually forget that he is a lion and what he is supposed to be. The next time you visit a zoo, go to the lion's cage and look him in the eyes. If he has been caged for years, he will not look at you.

Our society has become "pink" in many areas. Anything considered "dangerous" has to be tamed or dealt with to remove the danger. We see this approach toward males in our society, marriages, and churches. Because we have forgotten what a real man looks like, masculine strength is misunderstood and becomes a danger. Society produces a plentiful supply of boys but fewer and fewer men. Two reasons for this are that we don't know how to initiate boys into men, and we are not sure that we really want to.[4] William Pollack, director of the Center for Men at McKean Hospital made the following evaluation from his studies of the Columbine school shooting, "The idea widely held by our culture, is that the aggressive nature of boys is inherently bad, and we have to make them into something more like girls. The primary tool for that operation is our public school system."[5] Eldredge broadens this drift citing Lionel Tiger,

> "Boys as a group appear to prefer relatively boisterous and mobile activities to the sedate and physically restricted behaviour that school systems reward and to which girls seem to be more inclined. Many boys are diagnosed and medicated – the use of drugs is so disproportionately among boys betrays the failure of school authorities to understand sex differences...The only disease these boys may have is being male."[6]

A suppressed male who does not understand who he is supposed to be and understand his strength will never be fulfilled but will create problems in the search. Life is spent trying to answer his question by "proving" that he is a man. His avenues for doing that can be having sex with as many women as he can, exceling in sports, climbing the corporate ladder and having a successful career, acquiring large amounts of money, or just acquiring a bunch of "stuff" to show others that he is a man. All of this is a way to avoid being exposed, or having it discovered that he really does not feel like a man - which is his greatest fear. He hides, and like Adam, he finds "fig leaves" to cover himself to keep from being exposed. Men's hiding places are different, but a primary one is his personality. What he shows about himself to others is usually not close to what he feels on the inside. He will pick only the battles that he thinks he is sure to win – comfort zone battles.[7] He acts as if he knows what he is doing or talking about in numerous areas. A good example of this is a damsel in distress rescue of a lady broken down on the side of the road. He stops to assist, and the first thing he does is raise the hood of the car to take a look. Most men have no idea of what we are looking at, but it looks as if we do. Men have been spared the greatest insult to their manhood with the modern technology of the GPS. Now, we don't stay lost for hours only to bruise our pride and ask for directions! The fact is that we all try to hide somewhere or behind something.

Marriages can be a hiding place as well. It is typical for a man to marry a woman he thinks will not challenge him as a man. You see, most women don't understand what a real man looks like either, but she still has the need for one. She marries the man and immediately begins domesticating him, causing him to resent her. Then, she wonders where the passion went. This is where many marriages end up, regrettably.[8] One of the best hiding places for a man who does not really feel like a man is in the church. In most churches the "perception is perfection." Everyone is a "poser", so he doesn't have to fear being exposed. Be a nice guy and don't drink, cuss or smoke (in front of certain people) and be there every time the church doors are open, then you are a godly man! The image of the Christian man has conformed to the lion in the cage.

I recently saw this first hand when I was introduced to the father of one of our guys going through the Manhood class. He had a vibrant outgoing personality with Christian stuff on his hat and "oozed" Jesus in all of his discussions. He had a story of how "he" had prompted spiritual events in most of his relationships. He was exceedingly confident in quoting his strategic scripture. Behind his fig leaf and false self, was a trail of damaged relationships with his family, and pride that would not see that any of the material discussed that night applied to him in any way. One of our guys put it so plainly when he said that he wanted to see a man who could "live" the scriptures and not just "quote" them.

Jesus has even taken a beating in the taming process depicting Him as what I call the "Sunday School Jesus." He is very non-threatening and most likely he speaks with a British accent! Eldredge states it well, "The church has very efficiently pared the claws of the Lion of Judah, making Him a fitting household pet for pale curates and pious old ladies."[9] We don't want Him to be dangerous or violent, but the Bible tells us that He cleared the Temple, and will come back on a white horse to kick butt with a tattoo on His thigh!

A few years ago there was a book published that has also been made into a movie, *Heaven is for Real*. The little boy describes his visit to heaven with indisputable facts of who he interacted with while there. In the book, his dad kept asking him what Jesus looked like, showing him pictures of artists' rendition of Him. "Still, of the literally dozens of portraits of Jesus we'd seen since 2003, Colton had still never seen one he thought was right."[10] In his earlier description of Jesus, Colton said, "and his eyes, Oh, Dad, his eyes are so pretty!"[11] After his story became known, the father was contacted by a friend who told him to check out the story of a young Lithuanian-American girl named Akiane Kramarik, who lived in Idaho and had mysteriously been given the ability to draw after a heavenly vision. In her description of The Prince of Peace, "He's pure", Akiane said. "He's very masculine, really strong and big. And his eyes are just beautiful."[12]

The father explored the story, found the picture and showed it to his son. "What's wrong with this one, Colton? I said again. Utter silence. I nudged him in the arm. Colton? My seven-year-old turned to look at me and said, Dad, that one's right."[13] Now that's the Jesus I can get behind! He is a man's man. https://akiane.com/product/prince-of-peace/

The problem is that we misunderstand the meekness and humility that Jesus spoke about.

> Meekness is power under control. Humility is strong not bold; quiet not speechless; sure not arrogant. Humility is not denying the power you have, it is realizing that the power comes *through* you, not *from* you.[14]

Back to the Lion's eyes, I have asked my friend Mark to share his experience while on a mission trip in Africa.

* * * *

My name is Mark Bagwell, I pastored for 25 years and now my wife Sheila and I are missionaries leading an organization called Shade Tree Ministries in South Carolina. The ministry has afforded us many opportunities, one being a mission trip to Africa. During that trip, Sheila and I were literally 30 feet from this lion on a safari. One of the things that stood out the most was how he looked us straight in the eyes. It was moving and intimidating at the same time.

A couple of months ago, I shared with Sheila how I became angry, actually hurt by a call I received from a member of my former church. The next morning, Sheila shared that as I was telling her the story, all she could see in my eyes was the Lion because it brought her so much courage, joy, and understanding of God's protection and blessing.

Because there has been so much healing in my life as I have grown in my faith, the hurt feelings lasted only a few minutes. My wife also reminded me of how God has blessed us in the pastorate and now in the ministry that we stepped out on faith to launch. My strength comes from Jesus and not what man can give me. When I look into His eyes and experience His grace, then extend it to others, they see the Lion of Judah's strength as my wife pointed out to me that day.

I am convinced that Abba Father loves to give great gifts to his children and he is always watching and planning his next gift for us. As the old hymn says,

Turn your eyes upon Jesus. Look full in His wonderful face, and the things of earth will grow strangely dim, in the light of His glory and grace.[15]

*   *   *   *

In the book *The Lion, the Witch and the Wardrobe* when asked if Aslan was "safe", Mr. Beaver's response was, "No, but he is good!" This is Jesus and His masculine brothers. We don't need a "safe" Jesus because we are in the battle. However, He is "good." That should describe you and me as well.

Because he will behave better and not create as many problems, the stallion is made into a gelding by castration – emasculation. Though the act is not done physically to men in modern times, it is performed emotionally over and over again by society, in marriage, and our churches. Little boys are attacked early through our education system. There are no more strong men on our TV shows and commercials, Oh my gosh! The male is usually some bumbling fool that the woman has to help or just ignore. And then there is the homosexual agenda becoming ever present in the media that we are bombarded by each day. Tony Evans explained that if Satan can redefine the family away from its divine design, he can destroy the expansion of God's kingdom.[16] The man understanding his role and performing it in the family is the key to order and stability. Take the man out and things start breaking down. Sound familiar? You cannot teach a boy to use his strength by stripping him of it.[17] In many situations this is exactly what is happening to males in this country. Like the stallion, life can only continue to the next generation when you leave him as designed, so is the man. Emotional emasculation will stop the life that he was designed to pass along. So there you have it! Now you can see where we are in our society.

When Strength Goes Bad

When boys grow up and do not have their questions about being a man answered, their response is to become violent (physically or verbally) or go passive – Fight or Flight. Pay attention to this as you get to know men and it will be obvious how true this is. Men take this into marriage and parenting, resulting in our societal problems because there is no frame of reference other than how they were fathered. For most men, being "unfathered" is all we know.

Men know that something is not right but are not sure why they feel as they do. We have to ask ourselves:

1. How was your question answered?
2. Who answered it for you?
3. What are you hiding behind?
4. Where is your masculine strength being directed?

Whether we are aware of it or not, the answers have impacted:

- The man you are today
- Your perception of God
- Your approach to life
- Your approach to work
- Your approach to your family

Are you happy with the man you are today?

The Masculine Journey Map

John Eldredge developed the following stages of the masculine journey in his book *Fathered by God*. I have summarized them for you to see that there is a way that we should go in becoming a man. The problem is stated clearly in the Bible, *There is a way that seems right to man, but its end is the way of death.* Proverbs 14:12 NKJV. We have to do it God's way, or it will not work. I am going to let John's introduction set the stage.

> This is a book about what it looks like to become a man, and – far more our need – how to become a man…There is no more hazardous undertaking, this business of becoming a man, full of dangers, counterfeits, and disasters. It is the Great Trial of every man's life, played out over time, and every male young and old finds himself in this journey. Though there are few who find their way through. Our perilous journey has been made all the more difficult because we live in a time with very little direction. A time with very few fathers to show us the way.
> What you are holding in your hands is a map. It chronicles the stages of the masculine journey from boyhood to old age…The pleasure of a map is that it gives you the lay of the land, and yet you still have to make choices about how you will cover the terrain before you. A map is a guide, not a formula. It offers freedom…It tells you how to get where you are going.[18]

Stages of the "complete" Masculine Journey

- The Boy knows God as Father
- The Cowboy knows God as the One who initiates
- The Warrior knows God as the King he serves
- The Lover knows God as his intimate One
- The King knows God as his trusted Friend
- The Sage has a deep communion with God – a man living on heaven's shore[18]

None of the stages can be cut short, assaulted, unfinished, stolen in any way. We were meant to move on with the help of our fathers into the next steps of masculine initiation.

Dennis Rainey identified similar stages in his book *Stepping Up, A Call to Courageous Manhood* as Boyhood, Adolescence, Manhood, Mentor and Patriarch.

The point is that there are lessons to be learned from our

fathers, preferably, or other men in our lives, as we grow up. If it is not done or completed, there will be issues. Understanding the dynamics is key to moving on to be the man God designed us to be.

We must be intentional

All masculine initiation is ultimately spiritual. The tests and challenges, the joys and adventures are all designed to awaken a man's soul, draw him into contact with the masculine in himself, in other men, in the world, and in God as Father.[19]

At nearly every stage of our masculine journey, something in us needs to be dismantled and something needs to be healed. Often what needs to be dismantled is the false self, the poser, and approach to life we've created to secure ourselves in the world. What typically needs to be healed are the fear and wounds beneath it that fueled its construction.[20]

George MacDonald said,

> Our life is a quest, my brothers, arranged by our Father, for our initiation. There are gifts along the way to remind us that we are His beloved sons. Adventures to call forth the cowboy, and battles to train the warrior. There is Beauty to awaken the lover, and power on behalf of others to prepare the king. A lifetime of experience from which the sage will speak. The masculine journey, travelled for millennia by men before us. And now, my brothers, the trail calls us on. Remember this: *I will not leave you as orphans; I will come to you...My Father will love him, and will come to him and make our home with Him.* John 14: 18, 23 NIV. Because we are the sons of God, we must become the sons of God.[21]

One can easily see that the journey can be detoured at any of the stages but most critically as a boy. This comes at the hand of his father who does not understand what a real man looks like. The result is what Eldredge calls "unfinished and unfathered" men, boys in a man's body.[22] A majority of our societal problems can be traced back to a dysfunctional relationship with our fathers. It sounds too simple, but I have been observing and asking questions since I first discovered this, and every situation seems almost "textbook."

STEP 2 - UNDERSTAND THAT YOU HAVE ISSUES AND DECIDE TO OVERCOME THEM

Daddy Issues

I hold parents responsible for any sins they pass on to their children to the third, and yes, even to the fourth generation. Deuteronomy 5:9 MSG

Everyone has a father, so everyone has a "Daddy Story." It can be good or bad, or a combination of the two. Whatever your story, it affects who you are as a man.

The Way it's supposed to be

Masculinity is bestowed when a boy learns who he is and what he's got from a man or a company of men. He cannot learn it any other places - not from a woman and not from other boys.[1] We now see that boys are seeking affirmation from both because their dad tapped out or does not know himself. When a boy is raised by his mother with no male figure in his life, chances are that he will grow up to be a man just like his mother. The number of women raising boys on their own has grown to an epidemic number. I do not totally fault these women because they are doing the best that they can, but it is the men who need to step up. Women were not intended to be the father figure, but too many are having to try. We have to get men to understand their role and fill in the gap where the man has "run and hidden" from his responsibilities. Many women realize the need for their sons, but there are few men willing to answer the call to help. This has to change if our society is to be realigned as it was intended. Women have their own "daddy story" as well, contributing to the situation but, I am focusing on the men for now.

You see the plan from the beginning of time was that the father would lay the foundation for a young boy's heart, and pass on the essential knowledge and confidence in his strength. Dad would be the first man in his life, and forever the most important man. Above all, he would answer the question for his son and give him his name.[2]

Mothers and Sons

The father and mother have roles to play in the healthy development of a boy into a man. A boy is brought into the world by his mother and she is the center of his universe in those first tender months and years. But there comes a time for the shift when he begins to seek out his father's affection and attention. This is a very hard time in a mother's life of letting go, being replaced. Few mothers do it willingly; very few do it well. If a mother will not allow her son to become dangerous, if she does not let the father take him away (or if the father is not there to do it), he will be emasculated. A boy needs to be rescued by an active intervention of the father, or another man.[3] This is not a recent phenomenon because I recall people talking about "mama's boys" and being "tied to the apron strings" when I was growing up. In the stage of boyhood a "clingy" mother can upset the process.

I have seen how this happens, particularly when the son is the only man in a woman's life, and she clings to him with everything she has. The boy must pass into the world of men or he will forever search for his place there. A boy who is not released by his mother develops a bond with her that is like "emotional incest." Because they were not released, many adult men resent their mothers but cannot say why.[4] But God's Word tells us, *That is why a man will leave his father and mother and is united to his wife, and they become one flesh.* Genesis 2:24 NIV. This surfaced with my friend Russell during a *Wild at Heart* study and I have asked to share his story.

*   *   *   *

My name is Russell and I now understand that growing up without a father had a huge impact on my life as a boy and has followed me into my journey to manhood.

After getting involved with Rebuild Real Men, the Lord began to use my mentors as well as the material in books such as *Wild At Heart* and *Every Man's Battle* to shed light on areas of my life that had been dark for a long time. I began to see that some, if not most, of the poor decisions I had been making were my efforts to become a man. Unknowingly, I had been pursuing my masculinity in all the wrong ways. Though I have to personally take the blame for all of these less than perfect decisions made growing up, I believe they can be linked to a few underlying issues that were and, in some cases, still remain in my life.

In addition to the lack of positive male influences, coupled with the presence of bad male influences in my life, the effect of my mother's over-protective, over-bearing control on me recently surfaced as an additional contributor to the path that my search took.

As I entered middle school and began to make the physical transformation from a boy to a young man, my life really began to take a turn for the worse as I started using and selling drugs. I began carrying guns, fighting and engaging in all types of violent acts in search of my manhood. I became sexually active, having sex with as many girls as I could, as often as possible. These were all my efforts to feel like a man and dangerous, a feeling my mom never let me experience growing up. The large amounts of money, drugs and guns gave me a sense of power unparalleled by anything I had ever experienced. I thought I was well on my way to becoming a wealthy well respected man.

But these feeling were brought into proper prospective when I met Christ. After getting plugged into a church and being in the company of "real men", I discovered that everything I was doing was in fact "unmanly" to say the least in the eyes of the only One Who mattered. I was becoming the exact opposite of who I wanted to be and didn't understand the effects the terrible male role models in my life had on me. I feel so blessed that God has replaced them with positive males in my life, like the men in Rebuild Real Men.

Through these men, I have been able to understand and begin my journey away from my past as they spend their time reading books and sharing life experiences with me. The material along with the one-on-one time has helped mold me into the man I am today. I have been clean from drugs and alcohol more than 11 months. I have a job and go to college while being a father to my three boys. Thanks to godly men pouring into my life, I am able to give my boys a better example of what it is like to be a man. This is a vision that I was not given but have decided to break the cycle by having other men in my life to help me be a real man, husband and father to my family.

*   *   *   *

Breaking Tees

There is an essence of masculinity that is hard to describe but when you have experienced it, you know it as a male. Those of us who have been on athletic teams know about it and even as old guys, it is some of our fondest memories. Just hanging out with the guys fulfills a need we all have, to be in the presence of other men. I have heard it described as desiring "the smell of a man." Not in a perverted way, but in a wholesome passage of strength to strength. This early desire should be filled by your daddy. When a father and son spend long hours together, we could say that a substance almost like food passes from the older body to the younger. Boys love the physical contact with their fathers, to feel the strength all around them and to test theirs on him. This testing is so essential as they take you on a little at a time and the day comes when they can take you or inflict pain. This tells them that they have the strength like dad.[5]

My son Chandler has played many sports growing up and I am proud that I was able to be a part of it, coaching several of his teams. Golf is where we have connected and remains something that we can continue doing together in the years to come. As a young boy, he was fascinated that I could break a tee when I hit the ball with my driver. One of his goals was to make a ball mark on the green and the other to be able to break a tee. There is a large area behind our house that provided a great place for him to practice his "little-boy drives." One day I came home from work to find two broken tees on the kitchen table with a note "hey dad." This was a day in his life that he knew he had made another step toward being a man. He has progressed from teeing off at the 150 yard marker to the red tees, gold tees and then white and blue. He has made the ball mark and on his good days, out-drives me off the tee box. I can still give him a run for his money most of the time though! Golf has provided a great tool for him to realize the progress in his masculine journey and he has what it takes. If we had not had those times together, I would have missed "those moments" to speak into his young life "Yes, you are a man, and you have what it takes." We hear men talk about spending "quality time" with their children but life does not work out that way because time can rarely, if at all, be manipulated. You have to spend "quantity time" with your kids and be ready to seize the quality moments that present themselves in it. Boys particularly, like to talk when they are doing stuff. If you don't do stuff with your son, you may not have the opportunity of "that moment" to speak truth into his life. We only have one life and limited amount of "those moments" to speak into our children's lives. Two things that you cannot get back is time and words. *Carpe Diem* – Seize the Day!

So we see that there are two essential ingredients that need to be present for a boy to pass into manhood. His mother must let him go, and his father must take him away.

The mother's failure impacts the man, particularly when he gets married. But the "Father Wound" is damning for boys and girls as they enter the adult world with their question unanswered or answered badly. Actions and words or the lack of them shape a man's life as he seeks the answer to the question, "Am I a man, and do I have what it takes?" [6]

What Happens When It's Not Right

A violent father, physically, sexually or verbally says to the boy, "No, you are a mama's boy, an idiot, a faggot, a seagull!" These words came from a participant in the *Wild at Heart* video whose step-father said them to him, "you are just a seagull! All you do is sit, squawk and shit!" Without some kind of help, many men never recover from this kind of message. A passive father who may be present but silent or absent by working all of the time, involved in "more important things" or through divorce/abandonment sends the answer, "I don't know…I doubt it…you'll have to find out for yourself…probably not." Because these are subtle, they often go unrecognized as wounds and are more difficult to heal.[7] All of us have experienced this to some degree as we were growing up, no matter how good your life may have seemed to you. Because we live in a broken world, only sinful and imperfect people have children, so our parents were not perfect, no matter how hard they tried. It takes considerable effort to parent and we still don't get it all right even with a significant run at it. Assaultive and passive messages deliver a wound and our reaction to them shapes our personality in very significant ways. For some it can be misbehavior that cries out for involvement and engagement. For others it is a driven, independent perfectionism, while some withdraw from it all. The basic options for men to react to their wound is to become violent, overcompensating by being driven. The other response is to retreat and go passive. Some have a combination of the two depending on his circumstances. Whatever the response, the boy makes a vow, chooses a way of life that gives rise to the false self as his way of survival. For this reason, many men feel stuck, paralyzed and unable to move or unable to stop moving.[8]

The search for validation as a man takes us down many roads but the one most of us end up going down and the deadliest place is to the woman. We are still looking for Eve. Somehow, we believe that if we could find her, get her back, then we'd also recover our lost masculinity. Every boy has a time when it is crucial for a father to intervene (8-11years old) to be sure he is secure about his masculinity. Because the next window that opens in his soul is sexuality, if he seeks validation from a woman, he is set for a journey of disappointment. He finds a pretty girl who makes him feel like a man but when she breaks up, the process starts over in searching for *The Golden-haired Woman.*

> He sees her across the room, knows immediately that it is "She." He drops the relationship he has, pursues her, feels wild excitement, passion, beating heart, and obsession. After a few months, everything collapses; she becomes an ordinary woman. He is confused and puzzled. Then he sees once more a radiant face across the room, and the old certainty comes again. (Iron John)[9]

This was the path of my search. I always felt that I was incomplete if I did not have a girlfriend or dating a good-looking woman. My manhood was tied to the beauty of a woman and sports. There is nothing more beautiful and captivating than a woman's body. This is the attraction of pornography, making it the most addictive thing in the universe for men. We are bombarded by it every day with advertising, movie plots and the accepted "norm" of society – get the beauty, win her, bed her, and you are a man! A woman is a captivating thing, more captivating than anything else in all creation. Eve is a garden of delight but she's not everything you need – not even close. Femininity can never bestow masculinity so when a man takes his question to the woman what happens is either addiction or emasculation – usually both. Finding their Eve is a search without an end and a source of a lot of desperation in certain men and a lot of suffering women. Women don't want to validate you nor are they capable. If this is the goal, romance will turn to pressure and resentment. This truth hit me between the eyes to understand that if you give a woman the power to validate you as a man, then you also give her the power to invalidate you too![10] Thankfully, I never got trapped by porn but I know that if I do not guard that area, it could happen. Understanding your "areas" will save you much heartache over your life. Knowing where the punches will be coming from helps in the fight because you have a chance to duck or block them. Listen to my friend James and his journey down that path.

*   *   *   *

My name is James and the last five years of my thirty-year life has been an incredible journey. I am proud to say that I am well on my way to becoming the man God created me to be and understanding who I really am. However, it has been a painful road to recovery.

After hitting bottom and ending up in jail because of drugs and alcohol abuse, I entered a recovery program to begin the healing process. I had to deal with who I had become in my self-effort to numb the pain and it was not until I started looking honestly into my past with the help of other men that the healing process started. I realized that, as with all men, I had daddy issues despite growing up in a relatively healthy home environment leaving areas of my life "unfathered" affecting decisions that did not end up well.

As I unpacked my life, I thought I was dealing with drugs and alcohol but as we went through *Every Man's Battle* the light came on. I had been seeking comfort and validation from women. I began viewing pornography at the age of twelve and never had anyone to speak truth into my life of how it would damage me and my view of women, let alone tools for overcoming it. I just knew it was wrong but I liked how it made me feel early on and then became my "drug of choice."

I now realize that the drugs were an end to a means of women and sex. *Wild at Heart* helped me realize my search for masculine strength was being directed toward women. Finally the source of my struggle had been identified and I was given the tools to overcome the real barrier for growing closer to God which was lust for women. I am not where I need to be or want to be yet but I now have men in my life who can come alongside me and be there for me when I am attacked. I understand battles are not won overnight so I am not discouraged. This has been part of my life for a long time and will take time, effort and prayer to fully overcome. Understanding the sources of my actions has made me a better man in all areas of my life.

*   *   *   *

I heard a saying that "God looks after drunks and fools." In my case this is so true for both at different points in my life. Many times, we do not see God at work until we look back on our lives. Like I said, this was the path of validation that I took and there were many invalidations along the way. I finally found "the one" when I met my wife Jill one night after a mistletoe party at Clemson University. Her beauty was captivating and after our first date I knew it was her because of all of the previous dead-end relationships I had experienced. We spent hours talking and getting to know each other and I fell in love with her internal beauty as well as her external beauty. God had protected me all along my path and joined me with my soul mate even though I did not fully understand it all. A few months after we were married, I finally understood what Jesus' death meant to me personally and not just facts I had been told all of my life as I was checking off the boxes of religious activity. I accepted Him as my Lord and Savior and started a relationship instead of sin management. He has continued to direct my path and kept me married to my first wife since 1983, giving us three beautiful children who I am so proud of the people they are and are becoming. It was not until I realized that I was looking to Jill for my validation, however, that I reached a significant milestone in my masculine journey. Though I love her and need her by my side, I must see her as my partner and not the source of my manhood. That only comes from my heavenly Father.

Another avenue that men <u>and</u> women take with the "daddy issues" is homosexuality. The need for the masculine love is sexualized and the dead end road is travelled looking for it, leading to emptiness, heartache, and shame. I recently heard it referred to as a "legitimate need being met in an illegitimate way." God recently put someone in my life to help me better understand this path. Here is my friend Larry's story:

*   *   *   *

The year was 1951. On a summer day, Stella went to Clarence, her husband and said, "Honey, congratulations. I'm pregnant. We are going to have a baby." Just as blunt as the announcement itself, Clarence replied, "I don't know whose child you are carrying but it's not mine." Stella, my mom, was stunned. She was a virtuous Christian woman, and there was no room for anyone else to fulfill the fatherly role. Though cruel by some standards, these words of rejection set me up for the greatest privilege of all times.

Why on earth would my father say such a thing? To reject a child is one thing, to accuse your wife of infidelity is another. The Word says in Romans 2:1, "Wherein you judge you condemn yourself." God's psychology says wherein you judge you expose yourself. Time would later reveal many hidden factors and truths about my father.

But now, I was named Larry Eugene Lother. Mom took the initials from the doctor who had delivered me, Dr. L. E. Mays, and conjured up an adequate namesake. Little did she realize how the value and meanings of those names "Larry" and "Eugene" would become. My destiny actually depended them.

From my childhood, the absence of my father was quite normal. And even when he was present, the relationship was not a positive experience. Though forgiven now, I can vividly remember the intimidation my father delivered in hopes to "change" me. I was only seven years old. One day unexpectedly, he decided to mimic an incident that had happened days before. It was easy to remember my words and mannerisms that he was portraying. However, being a seven year old, I could only register mentally that I had been considered inferior -- soft, sensitive, and a sissy. His words and actions would result in seeds of rejection. Inferiority, based on comparison to others, became a regularity. I did not understand or relate to the disapproval of my father. Instead, anger, bitterness, hatred and unforgiveness were my constant reactions. His words were becoming the seedbed for my personality. I had no choice but to become resentful in my coping strategy to live in the same house with him. I found myself resisting to touch things he touched, like spoons in the gravy, or doorknobs he utilized to go into another room. If he touched a surface, I would wipe it off. If I followed him down a hallway, I would hold my breath to avoid breathing the air he breathed. It seemed I had no other choices but to hate the man.

Characteristics of meal times were daily harassments. It seemed dad would unload his frustrations of the day on me as though I was the culprit and cause. As I moved to adolescence mom was sympathetic to his abuse and would place my plate on the kitchen counter suggesting I eat in the den. I can never remember being chastened or physically disciplined by him. My memories were much harsher. For instance, I remember the day my sister brought home her newborn son just to hear dad say assertively, "Now, we have a real boy in the family."

School Life

During my elementary school years, I was branded occasionally as a "sissy" by my peers. Upon reaching junior high and budding adolescence, I graduated to being called every bullying comment from "homo", to "queer", to other names even less desirable. Bullying was an everyday challenge resulting in many physical assaults to the groin. Some days I would do without water just to avoid the "in crowd" who hung around the water fountain. Many times I would walk three hundred feet just to avoid the crowd. For the most part, I didn't even know what "sexuality" was let alone a "homosexual".

Male gender issues had never been assessed or affirmed. I coveted the friendship and acceptance of male peers. Oftentimes, I would become overly emotionally attached if anyone showed me the slightest form of attention. Strangely enough, I found myself becoming the words I was being called. Those words became a framework for the life I would live.

With the seventh grade came mandatory physical education. An athletic supporter or jock strap was required. It was just too intimate an object to approach the subject with my parents. Of course, there was showering in the nude after class. I found it to be both frightening as well as delightful. The age span of twelve- to eighteen-year-olds in the class provided full view and exposure to male anatomy. My curiosities were becoming attractions. Being in the state of full-blown puberty, it was not difficult to begin sexualizing my emotions. Neighborhood males became common visitors to my door. It was assessed that dysfunction was an epidemic on my street. Many homes were without fathers. Sleepovers were spent in exploration and fondling. Having another male touch my private areas was both stimulating and habit forming. Of course all the activity was done in secret. Though many of the other young men went on to lead productive heterosexual lives, my addiction was coupled with the rejection and need for male approval and affirmation. I was becoming more and more sexually attracted to other males. I did not realize the self-abuse I was committing in combining my imagination and sexuality.

I became emotionally dependent on several young men during this time. Weaving a web of manipulation would only produce heartache and depression. I kept telling myself, "If I could just be friends with this guy or that guy, I would be satisfied emotionally." I did not understand that no one can fill the place God has reserved for Himself. I was blessed by the grace of God to never do anything to the point that AIDS and HIV became an issue. These diseases were not even diagnosed or prevalent in society as they are by today's standard. During the later days of high school, I suffered immense depression and even considerable hopelessness and suicidal tendencies as a result of failed relationships. Many of my attractions were sexual in nature.

A paragraph from John Eldredge's book Wild at Heart says it well:

> Men who struggle with same-sex attraction are actually clearer on this point. They know that what is missing in their hearts is masculine love. The problems is that they've sexualized it. Joseph Nicolosi says that homosexuality is an attempt to repair the wound [Father] by filling it with masculinity, with the masculine love they never received or the masculine strength many men feel they do not possess. When the search becomes entangled with sexual issues, it also becomes a hopeless search and that is why the overwhelming number of homosexual relationships do not last, why so many gay men move from one man to another

and why so many them suffer from depression and a host of other addictions.

The Other Gender

Since the initial birth announcement to dad, mom always seem to have a chip on her shoulder when it came to demonstrative expressions of love. The question of her unfaithfulness was never resolved. She worked hard, both in the home and on a full-time job. She even occasionally took a nap before she would retire in the evening. Sensing that my older sister had the unmerited approval of my father caused more dynamics within our home and in my heart. It was not difficult for me to develop an attitude of distrust and disgust for women in general. As stated earlier, my need for gender identity and affirmation was not being met. Sex was a taboo topic and never openly discussed in our family. Passivity seemed to be the cure for the moment. Several convenience stores were within walking distance of our home, and they all boasted multiple racks of pornography. An occasional peek became the seedbed for a strong addiction. Though I began dating girls for social status, I was never physically attracted to them. Self-esteem was nonexistent and male approval was a constant necessity. I was an abused bullied individual.

Crisis Breeds Creativity

I was made to go to church as a child. My dad never attended but he made sure mom, my sister, and I regularly went to Sunday school and worship. Mom always let me sit down front on the second row. I was fascinated by the lady playing the organ. And though I never had music lessons, in later years I would become organist at the Full Gospel Temple playing the music "by ear." Mom also had a pencil and paper ready for me to doodle during hour-long sermons. Those markings became the beginning my path as a graphic artist. I was driven to gain popularity and acclaim through creative projects. Having won numerous national, state and local art awards, it was enough to keep me motivated despite the intense bullying. I used this new reputation to challenge the harassment. Numerous feature stories were written about my artistic ability in the local newspapers. I dedicated myself to all forms of creativity. I directed beauty pageants (though not attracted to the ladies), designed and built stage sets, designed commercial windows, business logos, and signage. Decorating homes inside and out for Christmas became a lucrative endeavor. Winning the local "Jaycee Outdoor Christmas Lighting Contest" was an annual goal and huge undertaking. Even more was to see my name accredited to the homes of other people who won. I did not realize how God was instilling a sense of self-esteem that kept me motivated. Though churched regularly, I did not have an understanding of God and his purposes for my life.

Arrangements were made for me to attend college and pursue a degree in Art. During a summer job, I injured my right hand to the point that college had to be delayed. My whole creative life was in jeopardy. During the period of rehabilitation, I became active and aligned with a local church. The Minister of Education and Youth, Philip E. Campbell, became greatly involved with my life. And though I was not a Christian, I was deeply intent on working towards God's approval – if I should ever meet him. I was fully aware of my sinfulness. Whatever I did on Saturday night would never keep me from achieving perfect attendance pins on Sunday morning.

Phil, the minister, was becoming friend, mentor and father to me. He was considerably handsome but his approval and acceptance far outweighed his looks. I was served and experienced unconditional love. Besides, I had never met any person who shared my middle name, "Eugene". Up until this time I somewhat had resented the name. The only times I had ever heard it was when my mom used it in disgust or disdain for me having done something wrong. I believe it was a divine setup. For six years, Phil kept me involved in stage and creative projects in the church. And though I had started my commute to college, I would go by the church daily to get my "fix" of acceptance and involvement from Phil. It was great to be accepted by his wife and children as well. Though I drove them nuts with frequent visits, I was always made to feel welcome. Triumph turned to tragedy when Phil was diagnosed with stomach cancer. After six years of his affirming friendship, Phil died in September of 1975 at the early age of 37. My world came to a halt. In his final days at Emory Hospital, Phil spoke a prophetic word that would alter my life forever. In his final words to me, Phil said, "God is going to do a miracle in your life." I had never discussed with him my inward struggle. God sure knows how to get the appropriate word to a person's heart.

Through Phil's death an intense vacuum was created in my spirit to know the God he knew.

Miracles?

Six months after Phil's death, I found myself suffering in severe depression from intense loneliness and lack of purpose. The church I attended hired a new minister that replaced Phil. And being new on staff, he wasn't interested in the ways things used to be done. I stood in my front yard, pointing my finger to the skies screaming, "Either you (God) make yourself real to me as you were in the Book, or I'm busting hell wide open." If there was a God, it was obvious I didn't know him. If there was a God why didn't he heal Phil? Why would a dying Phil declare a miracle over my life? My behavior was so compulsive. I needed a miracle. I needed a change from the inside out – a fresh start with understanding. I needed to be born again. According to counsel I received later, the moment I pointed my finger to God was the first moment I had sought Jesus with my whole heart. Little did I realize just how much He had engineered the moment.

Hadn't all my efforts been enough? I had dedicated myself "religiously" for six years. Going to church doesn't necessarily mean God is in the house. And all the works I did don't mean a thing when it comes to gaining entrance into heaven.

Then came the dreams. Intense, epic dreams that literally scared the hell out of me. I had dreams of Jesus coming back to earth as I was running in fear from him. For some reason Father allowed the right people to cross my life who had had intense conversions. I was developing a hunger for the Word of God, and my faith began to grow. The charismatic renewal was in full swing in the 1970's. Miracles and manifestations of God were becoming quite frequent and noted in mainline denominations. Catholics, Methodist, Presbyterians, etc., were experiencing manifestations of God's presence. John 14:21 promises

The person who has My commands and keeps them is the one who really loves Me: and whoever really loves Me will be loved by My Father, and I too will love him and show – reveal, manifest – Myself to him. I will let Myself be clearly seen by him and make Myself real to him. (AMP)

I was a homosexual but I had never admitted it. Believe me, many religious-minded people had insisted "I get right with Jesus." Their efforts just seemed to frustrate the whole process. You don't need to tell a homosexual that something is wrong and out of order. It seemed the only verse church-goers knew was that "homosexuality was an abomination to God." And they sure didn't show you the love of Jesus in their words of condemnation, nor could they show you the way to change from one status to the other. I needed the God who was real and able to make the change in my heart. Sad to say, even today most churches do not know how to approach the subject let alone know how to deal with homosexual matters.

Books, literature and Christian television were beginning to surface. Men like Oral Roberts, Pat Robertson, and a woman by the name of Kathryn Kuhlman, who had prayed for Phil, were forefront in my search. They all preached a message of faith and that God was still in the miracle-working business. My faith was ignited. In a three-week period, miracles began to manifest in multiple ways. God was guiding my footsteps. For the first time a new voice began to surface. It was the voice of the Holy Ghost speaking to my heart. I remember hearing him say, "I will not force myself upon you," leaving me to believe that it was up to me to invite him into my life. Change was a possibility. And on March 4, 1976, while driving my family's Buick, I repented. Pushing back the tears, I admitted for the first time in my life that "I was a homosexual." In my prayer I asked for Jesus to forgive me and to cleanse me from all my sin. Then I invited Him into my heart and I received Jesus by faith. I could see in my imagination when I reached out to him in faith, He came in. I knew for the first time in my life what it was to be born again. I was a new creature. Old things began to pass away. Compulsive behavior gave way to the restored power of choice when it came to temptation.

I will never forget the first verse and promise He made to me. So much of homosexuality was addictive behavior and thought patterns. The promise came from 1Corinthians 10:13:

> *There hath no temptation taken you but such as is common to man: but God is faithful, who will not suffer you to be tempted above that ye are able, but with the temptation will provide the way to escape, that ye may*

be able to bear it.

I never knew just how much He would help in the processes. And the second verse He taught me was just as powerful. 2 Corinthians 10:5 says,

Casting down imaginations, and every high thing that exalts itself against the knowledge of God, and bringing into captivity every thought to the obedience of Christ.

So much of homosexuality was in the realm of imaginations. Most of it is a deceitful fantasy world supported by our own sexual feelings.

Not only did the Holy Spirit instruct and lead me in the Word of God, but it was very evident He was empowering me as well.

But as many as received Him, to them gave He power to become the sons of God, even to them that believe on his name. John 1:12.

Sanctification became a reality as old habits, like masturbation, ceased. What had been a childhood addiction was now being replaced by a hunger and love for Almighty God. I used to struggle with looking at guys and checking them out. What a day it was when the Holy Ghost dropped into my spirit, "You don't have to look." God will develop within you the spirit of self-control.

I soon left the Baptist church and connected with a local charismatic assembly. I had gained a reputation for church pageantry and performance, so the opportunity to take on the 100-member church was quite favorable. The small church, under God's anointing, began to host crowds of 1500 to 7000 for Easter and Christmas performance. People even got saved.

The Opposite Sex

It was during this period that I became interested in the opposite sex. I had a desire to see the stigma of my past humiliation erased by a normal male/female relationship.

Father had more in store. I was 25 years old at the time. I will never forget the innocence and intensity in experiencing a normal erection upon embracing and giving a "good night" kiss to my date.

However, the following months became traumatic. For the first time I became public with my past. The secret was no longer in the closet. And the closet could no longer hold me from becoming the man I was supposed to be. Would I be accepted, or would I be rejected? Thinking that it would only help, I yielded to Father God so that he had the liberty to renew my mind that been bound by fear, anger and anxiety. I felt as though I was experiencing puberty all over again at the age of twenty-five. I firmly believe that my actual male sexuality and attraction to a female was latent inside. I went through intense anxiety attacks as well as insomnia for three solid weeks. When I confessed that I was losing my mind, Spirit-led counselors consoled me with the fact that I was being loosed from a mind that had been bound, shaped, formed, conceived, and practiced in sin and error. It became an intense time to

...pull down strongholds, casting down imaginations, and every high thing that exalts itself against the knowledge of God...
2 Corinthians 10:4,5

There was a "putting off of the old man" and a "putting on the new man in Christ Jesus."

My "God Mother"
Only God knows how to restore a person who struggles with SSA. I've often found that his ways are quite surprising. Number 1, if you're a male, you find yourself fascinated over other males. Number 2, if you're a male you're not interested in a female. The church that I was now attending expressed they had never had much success or seen success with those who came out of the homosexual lifestyle. Several men were super in becoming accountability partners, so the more I shared with them the less tempted I became. And then a registered nurse, Marjorie S. Day, stepped in to mentor me. Marjorie was a mother with three teenage boys. It so happened she had also taken several courses in psychology along with her nursing. Marjorie possessed spiritual depth and an extreme love for the word of God. She also had a gift when it came to writing letters of exhortation to others. All would prove to be so beneficial in helping me understand the paradigms of the past and the truths that would bring freedom

from my attractions. For more than six years as a friend Marjorie wrote letters to me, encouraged me, had me as guest for dinners, counseled me, and supported me. I can truly admit that she became a spiritual mother to my development. In turn, my anxieties and frustration towards females changed. Had it not been for Marjorie, I don't think I could have ever foreseen becoming a husband - a married man. Somehow when the spirit of a man reaches a certain maturity, the rest as far as soul, mind and body, get in line.

Marriage

Marriage is a God thing. After eleven years and three failed engagements, I found myself willing to die to the effort. However, it's when we give up and allow Him to work that His best plan comes into place. Within two weeks of surrendering my will to be married, I was introduced to the woman that I was told about prophetically eight years earlier. Gordon Gibbs, noted Australian prophetic minister, stated eight years prior to meeting Christina Lee Landon, "She will be a little older, but younger emotionally, but submissive. And don't be surprised if she has been married before." Little did I realize that Christina had "married" herself to God's call to be a missionary. On the first date with her I shared my past. She shared hers as well. On the second date we were engaged and married four months later. Three amazing sons and one grandson have been born to the marriage that lasted 30 years. Christina passed away on September 21, 2016, due to complications stemming from a stroke. My sons all know my past and are my greatest fans and support. By the grace of God, I would never want to fail or not live up to their opinions of me as a husband and a father.

Sonship - "Put a ring on his finger!"

I spent twenty-four years as a closet homosexual, struggling with identity, gender affirmation and same sex attraction (SSA). For the ensuing twenty-four years, I witnessed and experienced Father God bring a total restoration of my natural father. After thirty-three years of marriage to my mom, my father left, divorced and remarried. For four years my mom and I had a chance to rebuild our relationship that had a rough beginning. Forgiveness was the key that freed the Holy Spirit to move and transform the relationships. Strangely enough, I inherited the house and belongings my father had built and acquired. Having a son myself would make any grandfather proud. Before my father died on Father's Day in 1999, his wish was that I was to be given the sapphire ring he had worn for years. Scripturally, a ring is a sign of sonship illustrated beautifully in the return of the prodigal son. When the prodigal returned, the Father commanded, "Put a ring on his finger." Though the prodigal came back to become a servant, the Father insisted that "once a son, always a son." My Father had become my friend. We spent hours fellowshipping on his front porch. I was privileged to give my father's eulogy with no regrets. No one knew him as well as I had known him. Many healings and forgiveness's have taken place. I now regret that a relationship had been stolen, wasted and lost to error. Twenty-four years of wrong relationship was replaced with twenty four years of right relationship. I love my Father. In his own way, I know he truly loved me. I believe I will see my father in heaven.

Ministry

As you can imagine, having ministry opportunities offered to me has been a privilege through the years. I have served on numerous church pastoral staffs, licensed and ordained, and fulfilling much ministry travel. My greatest opportunity was becoming a chaplain at a local children's home in the area. My wife and I were also cottage parents to the high school boys at the home. We were blessed with a dozen young males who were in much need of a father. Night after night, I was privileged to sit and give to each of them affirmations that I had never been given. We even adopted one of the boys. That miraculous story is Part Two of this book. It's a story of faith and incredible works of the Father.

Father God has proved himself faithful throughout the years to keep me from falling. Though I've been tempted as everyone is, His truthfulness prevails in keeping me free from the past. Each day demands a denial of self and a condescending to Father's better way. Salvation is an ongoing daily process. Each day I have a choice to either do right or to do wrong.

Pornography was a challenge to overcome. God is ever merciful and patient as He works with me to *will and to do righteously His pleasure*. Philippians 2:13.

Unfaithfulness, adultery, divorce, even pornography were prevalent in my family generational lines. Father God can bring a person to the place that where what once was delight becomes distasteful. Pornography is a pseudo erotic pleasure based on untruth. *By the blood of the Lamb and by the word of our testimony...* (Revelation 12:11) we can overcome any addiction.

Victim to Victor

Day by day, the Holy Spirit reveals necessary truths that can assist in the "de-triggering" of past lusts and mindsets. New paradigms of righteousness and godly living can accommodate the hunger for an abundant life. I had been living my life as a "Victim" for twenty-four years. The name "Larry" means "Victor" or "Victorious Spirit". I was born to overcome. The fact that I was rejected while in the womb would become my greatest asset. The Word says,

When my father...forsakes me, then the LORD will take me up (choose me). Psalm 27:10.

In actuality, I was chosen in the womb, and my earthly father's negligence became my Heavenly Father's opportunity. And though I didn't understand this until I was in my early thirties, everything I missed was still available through faith. Jesus Christ is the transient of time. He's the same yesterday, today and forever. (Hebrews 13:8) What I had missed in my childhood ignorance would become a reality through His restoration.

I was chosen by God in the womb before I was ever born. The name "Eugene" means "well born, noble". 1 Peter 2:10 says,

But you are a chosen generation, a royal priesthood, and holy nation, a peculiar people that you should shew forth the praises of him who has called you out of darkness...

No longer am I a rejected victim. God's grace has produced a CHOSEN VICTOR!

You will show me the path of life; in your presence is fullness of joy, at your right hand, pleasures forevermore. Psalm 16:11.

You can become what God calls you. Now in my forty-three years of being set free, God continues to show himself faithful. My latest calling and activity has become mentoring men of all walks and persuasions. What Father God imparts to me, I can in turn impart to others.

For those needing help in being set free from Same Sex Attractions, please go to *HopeforWholeness.com*. Joe Dallas is a prominent figure in the ex-gay movement and has written a variety of books on the subject. His materials may be found on his website or through Amazon and/or local bookstores.

Larry Eugene Lother

*   *   *   *

There is support documentation written for both sides of this issue and I am not having a debate on it. Larry has helped me see that people going down this path are just looking for someone to love them. This is definitely a growth-area for me in developing a non-condemning view of the person whose sin nature is manifesting in a different way than mine. I recently realized that I may have turned the corner when I attended a wedding reception where there were two lesbian couples - obvious in appearance as well as their mannerisms. I actually looked at them through the eyes of love, wondering what the source of pain was in their lives that caused them to go down that path. There was a time in my not too distant past that I would have only had feelings of disgust toward them.

Some other resources that you might consider if you are not settled on this issue would be James Dobson's *Bringing Up Boys*. Dr. Dobson devotes chapter nine to it both from the clinical and spiritual viewpoints. Another resource is Dr. Joseph Nicolosi's materials that can be found at josephnicolosi.com . However, Paul covered it in 1 Corinthians 6:9-11 letting us know that this, among other sins, is not what people in the Kingdom do and that walking away from these lifestyles is part of the becoming the *new creation in Christ*.

I heard the best message on the issue of homosexuality at my church. It brings it from Jesus' perspective and addresses all sexual sin. People who are in homosexual and other lifestyle-sins are not experiencing God's best for themselves and deep down they know it. This is another empty place people take their wound and are either unaware or unwilling to admit what is really going on in their life.

Masculine strength is something to behold when properly cultivated and directed. The problem lies in that our strength is being misdirected because so many times it never gets on the right path to start with. We are in constant search for the answer to "the question" that haunts us. Each must ask:

1. What have I done with my question?
2. Where have taken it?

The answers will help us understand our issues and how to begin addressing them. We all have them, but the difference comes with recognizing them and taking a proactive approach to reconciling them.

In his book "365 Life Lessons from Bible People", Neil Wilson says,

> Our past may handicap us, but our own decisions condemn us. Understanding family problems and dysfunctions only becomes useful if we use the knowledge to make better choices. They can't help us if we simply use them to blame others for mistakes we are making. If we're smart enough to use our background as an excuse for our behavior, then we know enough to be responsible for our own actions. An evil past can be repeated or rejected for a better present."[12]

"If a problem has no solution, it may not be a problem, but a fact – not to be solved, but to be coped with over time."
~ Shimon Peres, former Israeli Prime Minister

Let's begin looking at these things in our past as a fact that happened and start dealing with them as such in order to get our masculine journey back on track so we can become the man God created us to be.

STEP 3 - SEEK FORGIVENESS FOR YOURSELF AND THEN FORGIVE OTHERS

"To err is human, to forgive, Divine." ~ Alexander Pope

In order to move forward in our masculine journey to becoming who God created us to be starts with forgiveness. Forgiving yourself and then others starts the healing process. Remember the Apollo 13 strategy? We have to acknowledge the problem in order to solve it. We have to identify it, deal with it, and move beyond it. When we see how things should have gone with our fathers, and most likely they did not go ideally, we may feel disappointment, resentment and anger.

Acknowledging these feelings and their sources is the initial step for moving beyond them. We have to understand that there is a wound to our masculine soul and it has to be healed. Most of the time we are taught as men to minimalize the hurt and call it "no big deal." We embrace it and just try to get on with life. How we handle the wound can be tragic and explains why so many men feel the way they do but don't know why. The hurt must be acknowledged and wept over in order to move forward. If we embrace it as just the way it is or feel that it was deserved in some way, we will never heal.

Understanding Anger

Anger is the emotion that most men feel over the wound in their masculine journey. Understanding anger and then dealing with it positively can be the key factor to overcoming chronic depression, sexual frustration, and relational breakdowns. It can be harnessed to help you grow personally, relationally and spiritually like you've never imagined.[1] This information has helped me tremendously in dealing with personal situations where I found myself angry, and speculating incorrectly about why. Now I understand more about anger and can better deal with the emotion and its source. The following material comes from a book and message series from Chip Ingram and Dr. Becca Johnson *Overcoming Emotions that Destroy*. Anger is a secondary emotion that indicates there is something wrong. It is neutral in that it can be both good and bad. It all depends why you are angry and what you do with your anger that makes the difference. Anger is a choice we make, it is not inherited from our parents or passed on down the family line. We express our anger differently, and Chip has broken them into three labels that describe how our anger "comes out." Their names tell you how anger is expressed:

1. Spewer
2. Stuffer
3. Leaker

He goes on to identify the main reasons that we get angry:

1. Hurt from unmet needs
2. Frustrations from unmet expectations
3. Insecurity from threatened self or self-esteem

We see from this that anger is only the tip of the iceberg with much more beneath the emotion. I realized that the source of much of my anger was frustrations from unmet expectations. When others disappoint you by doing things that you did not expect them to do or not do the things you expected them to do, this created frustration manifesting as anger. I also realized that a full plate and raising young children can result in frustration.

As you can see, everyone gets angry but it comes out in different ways. We all get angry for different reasons. But what we do with our anger is key. Chip summarized the ABCD's for what to do when you get angry.

A. Acknowledge you are/were angry
   • Admit and accept your anger – "I was angry at _____ when he/she _____".
B. Backtrack and identify the primary emotion(s).
   • Ask yourself what you were really feeling "What I really felt was _____ (hurt, frustrated, wounded, etc.)".

C. Consider the cause. (What contributed to the feelings?)
   - Ask yourself what happened and why you felt that way "I felt this way because _____".
D. Determine how to deal with it.
   - Ask yourself how did you respond to this situation.
   - Ask yourself what would it look like to address this anger issue in a positive way
     1. Talk with God about how you felt and why.
     2. Evaluate your response and apologize if necessary.
     3. Recognize that you were rightfully angry and that this good anger should motivate you to some positive response.

Here are some tools also identified in the book to deal with anger:

1. Communicate Needs
2. Communicate Frustrations – demands to desires
"I wish (hope, desire, would like) _____". (what I wish were different)
3. Ask yourself, "Why am I feeling threatened or insecure"?
   - What is under attack?
   - Who is attacking me?
   - Is the attack menial or meaningful?
   - Whose approval am I seeking to feel attacked?
4. Determine how to deal with it by asking
   - Who am I really angry at?
     ✓ Myself
     ✓ Someone else
     ✓ The situation
     ✓ God
   - What should I do?
     ✓ Confront or conceal?
     ✓ Will my plans make matters worse or better?
   - How do I deal with the situation?
     ✓ In person
     ✓ By phone
     ✓ Letter

✓ Anger discharge activities [2]

The brother of Jesus addresses the issue of anger, *Know this, my beloved brothers: let every person be quick to hear, slow to speak, slow to anger; for the anger of man does not produce the righteousness of God.* James 1:19-20 ESV
    I encourage you to get the book and read in more detail about the emotion that often stands in the way of moving forward in your masculine journey – anger.

    Anger can also be a result of suppressed grief. In our culture, it seems more acceptable for us to be angry than sad. Consequently, many of us stumble through life without understanding our feelings, completely out of touch with our emotions. We may be deeply grieved by a number of circumstances, but we don't feel safe acknowledging our sadness. It's socially "okay" for them to vent their anger, but not to explore and discuss the deep hurt beneath it.
    When you feel sad, anger seems like a safe retreat. It causes your adrenaline to rush. It commands attention and demands respect. It allows you to stay in control, and it keeps uncomfortable feelings and situations at a safe distance. However, your failure to grieve can actually poison you.[3]

What Forgiveness Is and Is Not

    "Throughout life people will make you mad, disrespect you and treat you bad. Let God deal with the things they do, 'cause hate in your heart will consume you too." ~ Will Smith

    Once you understand the emotional source(s) of your anger, the next step is to start the process of forgiveness. Forgiveness is a concept that is often misunderstood and so it is dismissed as an option in some situations. I personally struggled with it because I did not fully understand what it meant to forgive someone. The book *Boundaries* by Drs. Henry Cloud and John Townsend really shed a light on the concept and helped me move forward with a personal situation.
    Forgiveness is freedom from the past and the person who hurt you. It is not the same thing as opening up to more abuse. Nor is

it denying the wrong that you must name in order to forgive it. A wrong can never be undone, but it can be forgiven and rendered powerless over you. [4]

Tony Evans identifies three types of forgiveness in his booklet, *30 Days to Victory Through Forgiveness*. First there is personal forgiveness that many of us have never given. Shame and guilt can derail you from pursuing God's purpose for your life far easier than anything else. Satan uses our personal unforgiveness to keep us doubting ourselves and fosters the thought that we are not good enough for God to ever use.

The second type of forgiveness is unilateral where we extend forgiveness to someone who has not asked for it and may not have even repented of their offense.

Transactional forgiveness is the third type which is what we all seek. The offending party repents and asks for forgiveness and the process of reconciliation begins. Dr. Evans warns however, that before you restore a relationship with someone who seeks transactional forgiveness from you, take time to make sure they are offering true repentance and not just remorse.

He also shares that part of our forgiveness process is to seek the purpose God has in our pain. This helped me in working through forgiveness when I realized that what I was going through would ultimately help others when I shared my experience and process. I was relieved to read in this booklet that forgiveness is a daily decision and a process that will relapse from time to time. I have found that it is a great tool for spiritual warfare.[5]

Forgiveness vs. Reconciliation

The Bible says that we always need to forgive others (Matthew 6:16). However, we do not always achieve reconciliation with the person we must forgive. You see, forgiveness takes one person – it deals with the past. Reconciliation takes two people – it deals with the future. This was huge for me because I thought forgiving someone meant that I also had to reestablish the relationship with them but that is not the case.

Forgiveness by God's Design

You may say "wait a minute, you have to let them back in your life or you haven't extended Biblical forgiveness." Well let's look at the model that is all about relationships. God forgave the whole world but the whole world is not reconciled to Him – there is no relationship with Him. *I never knew you* (Matthew 7:23 ESV). People must choose to own up to their sin and repent, "then" God will open Himself to them.[6] It is very difficult, if not impossible, to give something that you don't have, so ask yourself if you have been forgiven by your Heavenly Father.[4] We may feel that we are not worthy of being forgiven but value is determined by the price paid (2 Corinthians 5:12). That is the great thing about grace – it does not depend on me to do anything other than accept the free gift of a relationship with God. All we have to do is tell Him we are sorry and want to move forward in the relationship with Him that is available through His Son Jesus. He paid the price so that forgiveness for sin is done – all we do is accept it by acknowledging it, apologizing for it then agreeing to move forward differently.

All relationships are based on trust and take time to establish. They require time to get to know each other and desire the best for the other person. A relationship is not always possible but forgiveness is a must if we are going to heal.

The following quote from *The Shack* that really summarizes this concept well.

> Forgiveness is not about forgetting. It is about letting go of another person's throat......Forgiveness does not create a relationship. Unless people speak the truth about what they have done and change their mind and behavior, a relationship of trust is not possible. When you forgive someone you certainly release them from judgment, but without true change, no real relationship can be established.........Forgiveness in no way requires that you trust the one you forgive. But should they finally confess and repent, you will discover a miracle in your own heart that allows you to reach out and begin to build between you a bridge of reconciliation.........Forgiveness does not excuse anything.........You may have to declare your forgiveness a hundred times the first day and the second day, but the third day will be less and each day after, until one day you will realize that you have forgiven completely. And then one day you will pray for his wholeness...[7]

This is huge for a man to grasp the idea that he can forgive his father but that does not mean that he has to have a relationship with him, particularly when he will not acknowledge any wrong on his part.

Pete Wilson author of *Let Hope In* was featured in a *Devotionals Daily* from *Faithgateway* titled *Breathe Grace*. He explained some concepts about forgiveness that furthered my understanding of how it works.

> In order to forgive, we have to truly realize the how we were forgiven by God. When we get that, when that moves from our head to our heart, we understand that we can't do anything but forgive people when they wrong us. We can't help but begin to let go of the hate that has us barricaded in the past.
>
> Hate is our natural response to any deep and unfair pain. Hate makes you want to see them hurt in the same way they made you hurt. It makes you dream about evening the score. We want the other person to get hurt back, to know the pain that they've inflicted on us.
>
> As we forgive people, we gradually begin to see them differently. Our hate blinds us, keeping us from seeing them apart from what they've done to us. But forgiveness allows us to see deeper into them. They were broken human beings before they hurt us, and they are broken human beings after they hurt us.
>
> To forgive someone is to let go of your desire to see them hurt. You let it go.
>
> With forgiveness there is a vertical transaction and a horizontal transaction.
>
> This is where we're learning to trust God, because we start with this vertical transaction. In an act of trust, we hand over the responsibility of what to do next to God. We fully acknowledge the wrong done to us, and we place both the act and the consequences into His hands.
>
> When someone hurts us, there are consequences. We're going to live with the consequences whether we want to or not. Our only choice is whether we will do so in the bitterness of unforgiveness or the freedom of forgiveness.

Forgiveness is me giving up the right to hurt you for hurting me. Instead of hurting you for hurting me, I make a conscious choice to free you despite hurting me. While hurt people will hurt people, free people will free people. [8]

Our Defense Mechanism

There is a way that seems right to a man but its end is the way to death.
Proverbs 16:25 ESV

From the place of our "woundedness" we construct the "false self", finding gifts that work for us and try to live off of them. They offer us safety and recognition that makes us feel good about ourselves. This can be focused toward academia, sports, career, or popularity. We just have the need to "feel it" for ourselves and from others. The imposter or false self is born as a defense against the pain; our plan of salvation. But what ends up happening is that those things we do to save our psyche, our self and to protect our inner life actually are what will destroy us. But the false self, our plan of redemption, seems right to us – it shields us from pain and secures us a little love and admiration.[9]

John Lynch describes it as a matter of trust. It has been proven to men over their lifetime that they cannot trust anyone. They come to feel that "if people see the real me, they would not love me so I will wear a mask so they will." The mask covers weakness, failure, or limitations that will keep people from loving them.[10]

I would like to introduce Tyler to you and let him tell a little of his story to bring this point home.

*   *   *   *

My name is Tyler. The only memory I have of the first five years of my life is verbal and physical abuse at the hand of my biological father toward my mother and me. While he was abusive when he was around I mostly feel abandonment because he was never there for me. I can remember him being gone all day, but he didn't have a job. Desiring male companionship with my dad, I would ask him to play with me when he came home. He would tell me that we would after I took a nap, but when I would wake up, he would be gone again. I had no idea of how this impacted who I had become until I was recently led to my past where I confronted it and grieved over what had happened to me. It was not a problem to be solved but a fact that had to be dealt with.

Because of my childhood situation, I grew up with many insecurities causing me to feel worthless, so I was a shy and scared young man. My mother encouraged me to hide my emotions, so I created the false self in order to survive. When my mother left my father with me, I began to formulate the new me (false self) who people would either be dependent on or afraid of. The hurt and fear were disguised behind fighting, I now know I was masking my desire for respect which never came, only more hurt, hate, and fear.

My next avenue to ease my pain at the age of 14 was drugs and sex. The drugs started as fun and then became an addiction. Seeking my validation from girls left me just as empty and addicted. I began to sell drugs which fed my desire for power to have people depend on me for something. For a brief time, I felt the power and respect I thought would make me happy, but it was short lived as it all came crashing down on me at the age of 19 when I was arrested.

I was allowed to enter a recovery program where over time the layers were slowly and painfully peeled away revealing the person hiding behind the fig leaf of shame and hurt. Through the power of Jesus and godly men pouring into me, I realized who I had become and how it all happened. My search for real manhood had been badly directed as a boy. I now know who God created me to be and am trying to allow Him to mold me into the real me and not the false self.

* * * *

Taking the mask off and getting rid of the false self is painful and takes some time. But you have to recognize that it exists and that it is a major barrier to becoming the man you were designed to be. We get comfortable with the mask, like jeans that have been worn several times and are molded to our shape. But underneath it is all the hurt and fear we've been running and hiding from. "Hiddenness" is always the first response to an awareness of sin. But we were not designed to hide but know and be known. We can only be loved to the extent we are known. We can only be fully loved if we are fully known. Drop the fig leaf and come out of hiding because as with Adam, The Lord God is asking "where are you?" He knows where you are and who you are but still pursues you so that He can have a relationship with you. He will do what needs to be done to clean you up and cover you up, all you need to do is come out, come out wherever you are!

We MUST Forgive Our Fathers

We are all individuals and just as there is no formula for a person to come to Christ, there is no formula for a man to get to the point of forgiving his father. That is why we have to grieve our wound. Grieving is a process that we go through when we experience a loss of any kind helping us get to a point of acceptance and a desire to move on. Eldredge outlined some guidelines in *Wild at Heart* for grieving our wound:

- ✓ It is not your fault and it did matter
- ✓ You have to allow yourself tears granted to the wound
- ✓ Years of "sucking it up" will melt away in your grief
- ✓ It is so important for us to grieve our wound; it is the only honest thing to do
- ✓ In grieving we admit the truth – we were hurt by someone we loved, that we lost something very dear, and it hurt us very much
- ✓ Tears are healing – they help to open and cleanse the wound
- ✓ Grief is a form of validation; it says the wound mattered
- ✓ We let God love us; we let Him get real close to us

If we do not move through this process, the bitterness and anger will be directed toward others – usually our wives and others closest to us. Forgiveness is setting the prisoner free and then discovering the prisoner was you.

In order to get to the point of forgiveness, we need to think of our fathers not as someone who has deprived us of love or companionship, but someone who himself had been deprived by his father and mother and culture.[11] Spend some time finding out what environment he grew up in and how he was treated and taught by his father. Sometimes, we don't know what we don't know. If you are a father, this comes easier as you know that you are doing the best that you know how. If your father was never taught how to be a good dad, how can he get it right if someone does not show him or unless he seeks it out for himself? This revelation was a huge turning point for me. As I was preparing the *Manhood* material, God spoke to me and told me that I needed to forgive my Daddy. From the outside looking in, we had what my sisters refer to a *Leave it to Beaver* childhood. Some of you don't understand this concept so *Google* it or ask a person who grew up in the 1950's – 60's about it. This was a perfect TV family where everyone respected each other and problems were solved in a positive manner in a thirty minute show, with commercials. In many ways this was true, my parents had a romance novel story, marrying weeks before daddy shipped off to the Pacific to fight Japan in World War II. After helping save the world, he returned home to attend medical school and to begin his family and practice as a rural doctor.

He was a great man who actually lived his faith every day in front of us and because of that, he was well-respected in the community and church. I grew up in an environment of warmth and love in a secure two-parent home. He was a great provider for our family, and our mother was able to devote all of her efforts to being a wife and mother. So you may be saying, "then shut up and consider yourself blessed!" Being the youngest of five, however, brings some dynamics to the scenario. Though I knew my father loved me, our relationship was "formal." I do not remember having "fun" with him even though he would take us places and on family vacations every year. There is only one time that I recall him playing with me. The rest of our time together seemed to be repairing fences and other chores associated with his "hobby farming." Tasks done were never affirmed as a "good job" instead "that's Ok, but I would have done it this way!" I don't know if he was just tired by the time I came along or if it was just the parenting style, but looking back I felt "on my own" in some areas in addition to not being quite good enough. My Mother had a little saying about Daddy that may shed some light: "He wasn't always right but he was <u>never</u> wrong!" My point on this is that even though I did not have a violent or abusive childhood, I now realize that there are still areas in which I was "unfathered." My father was already gone to be with the Lord when I came to this realization so I don't know how I would have had this conversation with him because of how much respect I had for him. He set a great example in many areas that I strive to emulate in my life. In addition to being a man of character and provider for his family, the greatest example he gave me was how to love and stay committed to my wife.

My mother died in June of 2008, and at that time Daddy was driving himself and doing the grocery shopping because my mother was confined to a wheel chair the last years of her life. Mother went into the hospital with internal bleeding that was diagnosed to be a minor situation and treatable with medication. However, her kidney's shut down and we had to watch her slowly die over several days as the toxins spread throughout her body and shut it down. The attending physician said, however, that this is a painless and peaceful way to go. After Mother's funeral, my Daddy basically gave up on living without his Dolly. Within about three months, we were feeding him and wiping his behind. He was in pretty good health, so it took until May of 2009 for his broken heart to take him home to see his Lord and his Dolly.

My oldest brother Harry took on a majority of Daddy's care during the week since he had his pharmacy in my Dad's clinic. Even in his declining condition, people still made appointments to come see Doctor Harry professionally. On the week-ends the other four of us would take turns staying with Daddy. I enjoyed these times and wish I could have taken this opportunity to talk with him about these things, but I had not grasped this information at that time. As his health continued to decline, I was called on more and more to help being the youngest and the only one who could physically handle him. I vividly remember one night when I put him to bed, as I was turning the lights off, he looked at me and said "Tiger, you know I love you?!" He had always returned the statement when it was said to him but never had he initiated it to me. I went to my truck and wept – at forty-nine years old, I had never heard my Daddy tell me unsolicited that he loved me! A spiritual mentor and pastor, Grady Long, told me that I had no idea what it took for a man from his generation to do that. As I was working through this material and reflecting back on my childhood I went to the emotional place I needed to go, wept and grieved over the missed parts in my relationship with Daddy. But I also realized that he was a human, doing the best that he knew how with a family that he loved. I wrote this in my journal on that day:

January 28, 2012
Daddy,
I forgive you today!
I know that you loved me and were proud of me even though rarely or never communicated, it was always demonstrated. You did the best that you knew how as I am trying with my children.
Jesus,
Heal my heart so that I can guide other men in seeking healing for theirs.

Forgiveness is a choice – it is not a feeling, but an act of the will. If your forgiveness doesn't visit the emotional core of your life, it will be incomplete. We acknowledge that it hurt, that it mattered, and we choose to extend forgiveness to our father. Forgiveness says, "It was wrong, it mattered, and I release you." And then ask God to Father us, and to tell us our true name.[12]

> Forgiveness is not an occasional act, it is a constant attitude.
> ~ Martin Luther King Jr.

But the problem comes in that the relationship with our earthly father forms the relationship with our Heavenly Father. James Bryan Smith stated it well in his book *The Good and Beautiful GOD* when he quoted A.W. Tozer,

> What comes into our mind when we think about God is the most important thing about us…Our thoughts about God will determine not only who we are but how we live…What we think about God – what we think God is like – will determine the relationship we have with God.[13]

I still feel "formal" with God at times and had a hard time with the concept of God loving to hear me laugh that my pastor used as an illustration one Sunday. I am still not there. My daddy was a man of few words so I had a hard time talking with him, it was only when necessary which meant there was a problem or I needed something. Wonder how my prayers have gone? Wes Yoder put into words exactly how I feel about my daddy in his book *Band of Brothers*,

> We admire him, but he was not available, not present even when he was with us physically, to help us understand how

to live…Still, we wish he had told us how, had given us advice and not waited for us to ask…We suspect our fathers knew something they could have told us but did not. Whatever it was they did not tell us, we wish they had. We see their limp, and we feel ours…A son wonders whether his father's silence means, somehow, that Dad did not – does not – delight in him.[14]

This is something that I still struggle with but I am learning by focusing on how I feel about my children. This understanding has brought me a long way in this area.

Grasping this dynamic is a breakpoint that all men have to come to if they are going to move forward in their masculine journey. Again, it is not a problem to be solved but a fact that has to be dealt with. Your father did teach you something – good or bad that you can build on. The Bible instructs us to *Honor your father and mother*. You may feel that he does not deserve to be honored. However, you will honor him by the man you become, whether you think he deserves to be honored or not. So keep moving forward in "becoming" the man God designed you to be.

Unforgiveness is a cancer that could be the thing that is holding you back in your masculine journey. I have heard it described as "drinking poison and expecting it to kill someone else." Your father may not know that he needs be forgiven by you and if you approach him, he still may not acknowledge or understand it. It would be great if you could have that conversation, he understood and cried with you, and you could move on with a great relationship from that point forward. The tragedy is that this rarely happens. You may not even know your father or how to get in touch with him, or he may have already died.

The great thing about forgiveness is that it only takes one. We can forgive our fathers without ever speaking with him because the forgiveness is for you. It should be a relief to understand that forgiving him does not mean that you have to open yourself up to a relationship with him making it possible to get hurt again. We have to take that step and make that choice. Right behavior is preceded by right thinking and you have to decide in your mind that there are things that you need to forgive your father for. I have encouraged men to write a letter to their father that may or may not ever be mailed. Getting your thoughts on paper really helps and is therapeutic to let the emotions flow. It may be at this time that you can cry over your loss when you feel the emotions that you have pushed down to avoid pain.

At my church, we talk about taking your "next step" in following Jesus. If you don't take your next step, you are "stuck!" There are men who live their lives "stuck" because they are unaware of the next step is or are unwilling to take it. As I mentioned earlier, in order to truly understand and extend forgiveness, you have to experience it for yourself. So I ask you "Has there ever been a time in your life when you realized that things with you and God are not OK because of your sin and you told your Heavenly Father that you were sorry?" If not, your next step is to get that taken care of. To do that you have to:

1. Admit that you are a sinner and separated from God (no relationship)
2. Believe that Jesus died for YOUR sins and then rose from the grave to give you the hope of eternal life
3. Confess Jesus as Lord of your life

If you declare with your mouth 'Jesus is Lord', and believe in your heart that God raised Him from the dead, you will be saved. For it is with your heart that you believe and are justified, and it is with your mouth that you profess your faith and are saved. Romans 10:9-10 NIV

There is no "right" way to do this but you just talk with your Heavenly Daddy and tell Him that you know you have never been reconciled with Him and you want a relationship with Him. You understand that He made it possible by sending His Son, Jesus, to pay that debt for you. And by accepting what Jesus did, you now want to move forward learning about Him and building that relationship with Him. Ask Him to forgive you and come live in your heart with His Holy Spirit.

Once you experience forgiveness for yourself, you can start the process of forgiving others – especially your father. Don't stay stuck here!

STEP 4 - UNDERSTAND AND PURSUE HEALTHY RELATIONSHIPS

Therefore a man shall leave his father and mother and hold fast to his wife, and they shall become one flesh. Genesis 2:24 ESV

It is not good for man to be alone

There is a lot of negative press right now on domestic violence, people are identifying the problem but not understanding its source or the solution. Tony Evans explains it perfectly,

> Government and civil laws are like cages in a zoo – they can restrain evil, but they cannot change the basic nature of the human heart. Art and education may refine the taste, but they cannot purify the heart. The holocaust was carried out by educated people, some brilliantly so.
> ~ Billy Graham

One of the most damaging things to the people around a man who has either lost his ability to breathe or is too afraid to try is that he becomes controlling, dominating, and either emotionally or physically abusive to someone weaker than himself. This typically shows up in a home between the husband and the wife. Although they may seem friendly, cooperative, and respectful at work, this man criticizes his wife, withholds affection, controls her spending and social life, and limits her personal and professional development so she remains in a constant state of forced dependency on him. He does this because he does not know how to feel or exercise legitimate power, so he seeks to dominate someone weaker than himself.

Legitimate power is power under the control and authority within the clearly defined boundaries of God. It is power surrendered to God's rule – first and foremost His primary rules to live in a way that reflects and manifests your love for Him and your love for others.

Men were created to breathe. Yet when society is the only one offering the gateway for breath, and when the gateway it offers is an illegitimate expression of manhood, the church has done a disservice to men. Because no greater legitimate authority for rule exists apart from God. And when men do not understand that they have been uniquely designed to lead within the domain in which they have been placed, they are left with a confusing definition of manhood that will wind up hurting not only themselves but also those around them."[1]

The majority of those trying to address this problem are women and through the female lens, the issue is not misdirected masculine strength needing to be properly channeled but danger that can only be detached by removing it from the male, by emasculation. This is a male problem that has to be addressed by males through a masculine approach. Signing pledge cards and making tougher laws only treat the symptom and not the source. If only this evidence of deeper problems in a man's life are addressed, it is like knocking a spider web down, returning to find it back the next day. You have to do something about the spider!

It starts with a proper respect for women's value. We begin in the Garden of Eden to lay the foundation. Women are the crown of creation, the embodiment of the beauty and mystery of God. God had created everything and had Adam name each one of what God had said was "very good." But there was something missing so God hit the pause button in the story. He had "spoken" the heavens and the earth into existence, He "created" the living creatures and "formed" man out of the dust "in His own image." But He took a rib out of Adam, the man, and "built" the woman. She was uniquely made and was the crown of creation. There is nothing in creation more beautiful than the woman but that brings her into the sites of the former most beautiful created being – Lucifer. Eldredge explains in *Wild at Heart* that she is the special target of the Evil One; He turns his most vicious malice against her. If he can destroy her or keep her captive, he can ruin the story.[2]

Women by God's Design

Every woman needs to know that she is exquisite and exotic and chosen. This is the core of her identity and the way she bears the "image of God." The Bible says that mankind was created in the image of God "male and female." I never thought about God having a feminine side until I read this material. We see how she bears the image of God in her desire expressed through the questions that she seeks to have answered, "Will you pursue me? Do you delight in me? Will you fight for me?" If these questions are not answered by her daddy, she will spend her life trying to get them answered and at a very high cost.[3] The assault on her continues as she grows up through violent and passive men who emerge from her unanswered question. The tower is built brick by brick and when she is grown it can be a fortress. If her father is a passive man, she will suffer a silent abandonment. Women need a lover and warrior, not a really nice, hesitant guy.[4] But hesitancy is what we inherited from Adam. God told Adam not to eat the fruit after he placed him in the garden, right before He created the woman. It was his responsibility to lead and protect, but when the serpent started talking to his wife he did not fulfill his role. The Bible says that after the woman dialoged with the serpent that she ate the fruit and "gave some to her husband who was with her." Adam was right there the whole time and hesitated, and the world has never been the same.

There are other men in the Bible who, when it came time to fight, hesitated. We want to look like a knight but we don't want to bleed like one. We don't understand the tower, the dragon, or what our strength is for. The number one problem between men and their women is that we men, when asked to truly fight for her, hesitate. We are still seeking to save ourselves and have forgotten the deep pleasure of spilling our life for another. When a woman never hears she's worth fighting for, she comes to believe that's the sort of treatment she deserves. It is a twisted form of attention but she rationalizes that it is better than nothing.[5] This is where a father is so important in a woman's life. If she never experiences being treated like a lady and never observes what a real man looks like, she will settle for crumbs. Having a father who is there loving her mother and showing her what respect looks like will set the standard as she seeks her prince.

Your Strength by God's Design

A key to moving forward in our masculine journey is to understand masculine strength and its designed purpose. All of creation points to a larger picture in its design if we will just look closer. This is revealed in *Wild at Heart* with the following quote to help show what we were given our strength for.

> Our sexuality offers a parable of amazing depth when it comes to being masculine and feminine. The man comes to offer his strength and the woman invites the man into herself, an act that requires courage and vulnerability and selflessness for both of them. Notice first that if the man will not rise to the occasion, nothing will happen. He must move; his strength must swell before he can enter her. But neither will the love consummate unless the woman opens herself in stunning vulnerability. When both are living as they were meant to live, the man enters his woman and offers her his strength. He spills himself there, in her, for her; she draws him in, embraces and envelopes him. When all is over he is spent; but ah, what a sweet death it is.

Going back to the stallion analogy, our masculine strength is the life that we have to offer. When a man withholds himself from his woman, he leaves her without the life only he can bring. This is never truer than how a man offers or does not offer his words. Proverbs 18:21 tells us that *the tongue has power of life and death*... Words from a father or husband can destroy or starve a woman. A violent man destroys with his words and a passive man starves with the lack of words.[6] So we need to be careful how we speak to our daughters, wives and girlfriends as well as the other women in our sphere of influence.

Using Her

When men do not understand the value and strength of women, the Evil One uses us to continue his assault. Sex sells, and society has slowly accepted the "objectification" of women for companies to market their products. Pornography and even advertising has made the beauty and captivation of a woman's body "something" desired instead of "somebody" to get to know. Most men want the maiden without any sort of cost to themselves. They want the joys of the beauty without the woes of the battle.[7] All we have to do is turn on the computer screen, watch TV or look through the paper or magazine and we get the thrill of a woman without having to fight for her. In their Every Man series, Stephen Arterburn and Fred Stoeker explain that because men are visual, we can get the thrill by just looking or thinking. We get the chemical rush that sexual relations provide without ever interacting with a female. Even if nothing is available to look at, we can go back and pull it out of our memory. Women may be able to think with both sides of their brains and multitask well but guys can recall images of beautiful women and sexually stimulating thoughts from many years back. As I told you earlier, pornography was not a road that I went down but I was exposed to it. The first time was at the age of thirteen years old when a man in our neighborhood told us "you boys are old enough to see this" as he pulled out the hard porn magazines. This was not a *Playboy* or even *Hustler* but zoomed-in intercourse! We thought it was great as thirteen year old boys and knew that we had arrived as men by getting to look at it. But now I know that this man was struggling in his manhood, turning to alcohol and constant sexual encounters to ease his pain. That was in 1973, and to this day I can still see those images when I am attacked spiritually. Women never forget stuff that was said or done, but men never forget what they see.

Pornography is what happens when a man insists on being energized by a woman and uses her to get a "feeling" that he is a man. This is a false strength and a model of selfishness because he offers nothing and takes everything.[8] Because pornography is so available now, it has become an epidemic addiction for many males. Pornography crosses the age as well as socio-economic barriers in its addictive grasp. I served as a leader for our church's summer student ministry trip to Daytona Beach. We take a large number of students, middle school and high school to the beach for a week of intense Bible study and fun. I was assigned to room with three middle school boys at the 2013 trip. The first night our pastor confronts them with their salvation experience – "are you saved or not?" After the worship service we go back to the room and "unpack" the message. On previous trips, I had always had one in the group who had not accepted Christ and the week was focused on helping him see the need for a relationship with God and how to have one. This group of boys were going into the eighth grade, saved and growing in their walk. I thought to myself, "Well I guess I just squirt oil on the machines to make them run faster." One of the young men reminded me of Wally Cleaver with his demeanor and mannerisms. He had his own lawn care business with money in the bank! Wednesday night is "the talk" night where the topic is sex. During the invitation, Wally stood up. I ran through all of the scenarios in my mind but when we got back to the room for group time, he shared that he was addicted to pornography. After his Dad, who he lived with, went off to work each morning he looked at porn on the computer before he began his day cutting grass. Whoa! That was about the same age that I was introduced to it but I did not have the internet. This is a huge problem for many males that is not easily shared. It remains hidden because of the perception that it is perversion instead of addiction. My friend Tim went down this road, and here is his story of where it took him.

*   *   *   *

The sound of the handcuffs cut through the silence of my shocked daze. Click. Click. Tick-tick-tick. Click. "How could this happen to me? I told myself over and over. How could this happen to me? I've just lost it all. I've lost my wife, my children, my career." I had spent my whole life cultivating the image of the perfect churchman. As the music minister of a small Baptist church, my life was as much about performing as preparing my choir to sing pitch-perfectly to Jesus every Sunday for more than 30 years. My suits were sharp, and my shirts starched. My hair was styled and trim; not a hair was out of place. Even my home's front lawn was manicured and my bushes groomed. If one of my congregation drove by the house, nothing could distract from the perception that my life was in order, always under control. Perfect.

And here I was pulled out of my truck in a seedy park in a neighboring town, busted by undercover police. I'd found the place on Craigslist a few weeks before. Curious, I'd driven up a couple times and left. But this time I parked. And when I was offered sex, a simple *yes* was all it took to undo all the stitches and seams of my meticulously tailored life. I was exposed. A dark, sinful lust I could never control had finally come to light, just as Jesus promised in the Bible it would. With my mind racing in a million different directions, everything going on around me was a muffle and blur. But as I was being led away by officers, I heard the words of a voice — the voice I knew was God's — loudly and clearly. "Enough is enough."

I grew up the son of Williamston millworkers, pillars of their local church, who wanted nothing more than for my older brother and me to dedicate our lives to serving God. At 15, I asked Jesus into my life. But my relationship with God was always suffocated by secrets and lies until my public humiliation led me to NewSpring Church in 2010. That's where God's grace and forgiveness began to flow into my life, and where I discovered my true ministry. As painful as that life crash was, I wouldn't go back and change history, even if I could. The best way to honor God is to be an example of His grace. I now see people as He sees me: broken but worth redeeming.

My sexual addiction started as a teenager, when one of the boys I was running with in the mill village showed me the creased, torn-out pages of a magazine stolen from a parent's pornography stash.

Then I suffered sexual abuse at the hands of a neighborhood man the summer between my seventh and eighth grade years, which only added to my sexual confusion. I didn't understand what had happened to me. When I told my parents of it, the dumbfounded silence left me feeling guilty. "Maybe I'd done something wrong?"

When my wife of 35 years, Stacy, and I were still newlyweds, I happened to mention the abuse in casual conversation. I blew off Stacy's suggestion that I speak to a counselor. "Junk like that happens to everybody all the time", I remember telling her. "It's not a big deal." This is how most men handle childhood pain in order to avoid dealing with it. I discovered how wrong I was in a sexual addiction treatment center a week after the arrest. I wept uncontrollably and continuously for days as I came to terms with the pain I'd buried for so long. "The wound", no matter what form it is in, has to be wept and grieved over in order for healing to take place.

For 30 years, my career in ministry had been my ultimate cover story. After graduating from the music ministry program at then Anderson College, I found church after church that was eager to hire me for my musical gifts and polished personality — first part time and then full time. But Jesus was never the focus. All the years I was in ministry, I knew I was saved, but I kept my face turned from God. The reason I was a perfectionist and the reason I worked hard being so polished...was that if I was perfect, who could question my morality? I worked hard at being perfect. I didn't want anyone to question me in any way. I knew my addiction to porn was displeasing and dishonoring to God, but I thought that if I do my very best that I can possibly do for God, surely he won't mind. I can't tell you how much I prayed, crying out to God, promising God, making deals with God. "Help me with this." Only you can take it from me, and that lasts two or three days, and then you're right back in front of a computer doing the same old thing again.

When I returned home from my six-month stint in treatment, I discovered that Stacy and my two children had chosen to seek refuge at NewSpring, a place where "no perfect people are allowed." I knew I needed to be part of a church to faithfully follow Jesus with all my heart. "Where else would have me?" I told myself. It was on my first visit to NewSpring the pastor happened to mention that he, too, had struggled for years with pornography. And I knew I was in the right place to heal.

For a long time, the shame and embarrassment remained so strong that I wouldn't go to my hometown grocery store or post office. I'd stick to the back streets when driving through town. That was until one day when I heard the pastor say "you are who you are in Christ. No matter what people may think I am, I am who I am in Christ, and that's all that matters." That totally revolutionized my life and now I don't let shame govern my behavior. Despite my public shaming in newspapers and television, Stacy and I first volunteered welcoming new guests — a perfect outlet for our gifts God had given us.

We found overwhelming love and acceptance in our community of volunteers and in our NewSpring Group. They not only knew of our imperfections but embraced them as a testament to how God can change and make things new. And just when I thought my life in ministry was over and done, I discovered the best was yet to come. We eventually took on more leadership roles in other areas of the church. And in September 2014, I was hired to be the Next Steps Director at NewSpring Boiling Springs campus. Jesus chose to use those who were down and out. All the main characters in the Bible were broken. When He uses those people, it can't be explained aside from God, and He gets the glory.

As a volunteer in the Care Room and at Next Steps events at

church, I found myself in countless conversations with men who have struggled long and silently with an addiction to pornography, just as I had. When I'm talking to men now, I know firsthand they never could imagine how far their secret shame and compulsion could take them into darkness. And I know they could never anticipate how much devastation it would cause to their wives and children. Only by God's mercy was my wife able to stand by me through the utter humiliation. She prayed that God would give her the forgiveness she needed to offer, and that God would allow her to see me as He does. Though unpopular to most of those close to her, she chose to honor her marriage commitment to me, for better or for worse.

When I share my story, I still feel shame and embarrassment. But offering the hope of Jesus is worth it. I am proof of how much forgiveness and grace Jesus has for His children. Bring sin to the light. That's the first step in receiving God's forgiveness, and the power to overcome temptation. Being broken is the beginning of being made whole. I was forced out of the shadows but please don't wait for that to happen to you if this is an area you are struggling with. Tell someone that you trust to walk alongside you and hold you accountable. The pastor shared that his first step to being healed of this cancer was to tell a friend and bring it into The Light.

Jesus is now firmly at the center of my life. Freed from the chains of addiction and the weight of years of pretending, I am experiencing joy in my life like never before. My marriage grew stronger. There are no longer any lies or secrets between us, and it is precious that our children have grown spiritually watching us work through this. You can have this freedom and restoration too. But if you stay in the shadows, it will never become a reality for you.

In all my time as a music minister, I'd never led a single person to Jesus. But since being forgiven and restored by God's grace, I've been part of many conversations that have resulted in people asking Jesus into their lives! Having been through what I've been through, I'm absolutely blown away that God would use me. I spent the first half of my life trying to please everybody, and I plan to spend the rest of my life pleasing Him.

* * * *

All Pro Dad published the following information related to pornography.

Pornography Statistic Sources
1. 25 percent of all search engine requests are pornography related [9]
2. For every 10 men in church, 5 are struggling with pornography [10]
3. Median age for the first use of pornography: boys: 11-13 girls: 12-14 [11]
4. According to 2004 IFR research, U.S. porn revenue exceeds the combined revenues of ABC, CBS, and NBC (6.2 billion). Porn revenue is larger than all combined revenues of all professional football, baseball, and basketball franchises. The pornography industry, according to conservative estimates, brings in $57 billion per year, of which the United States is responsible for $12 billion. [12]

    We are slowly realizing that it is an addictive behavior that men and now women turn to self-efforts to ease the pain. There are chemical reactions with viewing pornography that offer a brief comfort but like all other addictive behaviors, most have remorse after the feeling wears off. It was shared with me that men who grow up in a strict religious environment tend to turn to porn because it is so easy to hide, unlike alcohol or drugs. A doctor once told me that people will spend money to experience pleasure or avoid pain. Pornography offers both.
    Because of this course our culture has taken, women are abused in that they are pursued - but not really; they are wanted - but only superficially. A woman who does not understand her true beauty learns to offer her body but never her soul. This superficial relationship thrives because men never get their question answered and feel that if they offer all that they have to a woman, it will not be enough. But a woman needs to have her sense of worth from another source than a man just as we need our validation from our Father. [13]
    We don't know how long Adam was asleep while God "built" the woman but it needs to be noted that she spent time with her Heavenly Father and had a relationship with Him "before" she was walked down the aisle and given away to her husband. A women

needs have a good relationship with both her earthly and most of all her Heavenly Father to be at her best. A woman at her best will arouse, inspire, energize and seduce her man! [14]

Size *Does* Matter - Feminine Mistrust

I love it when I get a word from God and the following information cannot be explained any other way. Long-time friends of ours agreed to host a *Manhood* class at their gym. We decided to have t-shirts made up to create an interest for future classes we hoped to have. The strategy was for the guys who went through the class to work out in the t-shirts and have conversations when people asked about them. A long-time point that I had humorously (but seriously) made was about the logo for the gym. It is a "bull" with the suggestive slogan, "Size Does Matter", under it but with closer examination, the animal is really a steer. I told her that if we were going to make up shirts and talk about being a man, it had to be anatomically correct! She reluctantly agreed and I was off to have the t-shirt designed. The first concept was forwarded to both of them, since they were paying for the shirts, and the response from her was "they're too big!" Almost taking the avenue of seeking forgiveness instead of permission, I was cutting my grass when God spoke to me with the thought that there was more to it and I needed to look for the lesson. I often "hear" from God while cutting my grass so I call this one of my "John Deere" moments.

I did a quick internet search for the definition of testicle which means in Latin "witness of virility." Well that was great but I needed to know about virility defined as "man or manly; masculine characteristics viewed positively; marked by strength or force; commonly associated with vigor, health, sturdiness and constitution." It means "a visual representation of masculinity!"

Whoa! The message was that when a woman does not trust a man to use his masculine strength in the designed way, she will "govern or cut it off" to avoid being hurt by him. Though we read about the occasional situations where it is tried physically, how often does it happen emotionally? Little girls who never learn to trust the males in their life, grow into a women who do not trust men – some justifiably so.

I have asked my friend, Bryan, to share his experience with this revelation.

* * * *

A Basset Hound or a Marriage Before 40

Through life decisions and events, I had remained unmarried at the age of 35. No big deal really, I had dated a few times but I wasn't in a hurry to get married. But at that age, I figured that I should at least set some life goals, and this is what I came up with. By the time I was 40, I was going to either own a basset hound or get married. Pretty lofty goals for someone who always had a family dog, but had never raised one alone and thought I was ready to find the "perfect woman" when I wasn't dating anyone seriously.

Let me back up a few years, and explain how I got to that point in my life. I became dependent on alcohol in my mid-20's, to the point where it was affecting my family, school, friends and relationships. My view on life was continually clouded by periods of drunkenness, blackouts, hangovers and everything in between. Relationships were initiated in bars, and usually ended in excuses to drink even more. I didn't know what a real relationship was. By the Grace of God, I decided at the age of 32 to get help, and have remained sober for 24 years.

Learning to make better life decisions, and presented with clarity, I was resigned to the fact that I was probably not going to get married by 40, so I obtained a Basset Hound puppy, and reached that life goal at 41. By chance, I met a woman who had previously been married and had a daughter. I already had my Basset Hound, so hey, why not? We had dated for some time, thinking that I knew what it takes for a healthy marriage, we got married, bought a house and planned on living happily ever after. After 8 years of marriage, we divorced and went our separate ways.

What happened? A few things really. Love was not part of the relationship or marriage, and it really wasn't until I took the *Manhood* class as part of ReBuild Real Men that it hit me that I was not allowed to be a real man. I spent eight years trying to be someone that my then-wife wanted me to be; not sure what it was, but through the *Manhood* class and support, the moment of clarity was huge. I had my manhood taken away, "cut off", by my wife who did not know what a real man looked like nor know how to trust a man because of her life's journey. I allowed it to happen because I did not know either! I can go back in my life and point to things that did or did not happen, but those are just excuses. What I did not have was a personal relationship with God, that I now know is guiding me in my journey in becoming real man. My Basset Hound recently passed away, but my journey with God is teaching me how to be a real man in a real marriage. I am finally reclaiming my manhood and understanding that "size does matter!"

Bryan L. Hoover

*　　　*　　　*　　　*

I went back to the designer, had him "pull them up a little", and prepared to review the new proof with her. God sent me to Ephesians 5:25-28 which in the Message translation speaks beautifully how our masculine strength is to be used,

> *Husbands, go all out in your love for your wives, exactly as Christ did for the church – a love marked by giving, not getting. Christ's love makes the church whole. His words evoke her beauty. Everything he does and says is designed to bring the best out of her, dressing her in dazzling white silk, radiant with holiness. And that is how husbands ought to love their wives. They're already one in marriage.*

I read it to her and explained the symbolism that I had discovered then asked, "If the size is an indicator of how a man uses his manhood putting this into practice, how big should they be?" After she thought about it a minute she said, "They should be real big!" We went ahead with the modified design and this story was added to the *Manhood* class and is now in this book.

Many men like to pull out the Ephesians passage where it talks about wives submitting to their husbands and they fail to read on and understand what Paul was saying. In their book *Every Man's Marriage*, Stephen Arterburn and Fred Stoeker explained it so well in that

"Jesus submitted, through suffering and death, to oneness with us. He laid down His life in full submission for the sake of our relationship with Him, though we were sinners. Only then did He ask in return for our full submission to His authority. His submission to oneness and our submission to His authority made oneness possible. Oneness always requires mutual submission." Continuing by quoting a woman whose husband gets it, "If Bill is fulfilling his role to me as Christ loved the church. He'll be unselfishly seeking my best. His expectations will be reasonable, and he'll make decisions with the highest good for our family in mind. For me, submission to Bill is almost a reflex because I trust him so." [15]

You see if our masculine strength is properly understood and displayed, there are no limitations on its size. Show your manhood in a "big" way. And with that thought in mind, remember that "Size <u>does</u> matter!"

Will You Fight For Her?

We must act like a warrior and step between her and the forces of darkness that are coming against her – take on the dragon! Remember that she is under a special attack from the evil one. This cannot just be a one-time event or every now and then, we must be in it for good and see this as a hill worth dying on. "The universe is so vast and so ageless that the life of one man can only be justified by the measure of his sacrifice."[16] Satan does not want your marriage to succeed and is relishing in its failure, doing what he can to create problems for both of you so that you do not make it or have a chance of reclamation.

Here are the words of a female broken heart feeling abandoned and not fought for written by my daughter Olivia to her now husband John after they broke up early in their relationship.

* * * *

It has taken me a lot of time to start to sort out my thoughts and feelings about this whole situation, and I have such a long ways to go, as I am only beginning to actually feel or think anything in particular this last week. I have been emotionless and thoughtless, partly because I am consciously suppressing my emotions and partly because I am so confused by everything that has happened. I have been lost in my own head, not knowing who to turn to, or what to do with myself...and am just now allowing myself to feel the raw emotions of this break up. I feel like you need to know some of my thoughts and feelings and I apologize if they are jumbled and incomplete.

I decided to read *Captivating* this weekend and it has helped bring words to my emotions that I previously couldn't explain to anyone. It is obvious to say that I am hurt. You and I had something that I had never felt before in my life. I have been lonely all my life in waiting for someone to come along and love me for my offerings and beauty that my dad has always told me I had. Deep down I knew he was right, but the long years of not having someone recognize and enjoy my beauty openly had caused my walls to build up and my vulnerability to hide behind sarcasm and a confident, expressive personality. When I met you, you were a pleasant surprise...I enjoyed talking to you and found we had so much in common I found myself wanting to learn more about you. As time passed you showed me a soft side, a side that seemed truly intrigued by me and my beauty, and you always made a point to tell me those things, in the soft loving words you spoke, or the small acts of kindness. You made me feel special and worth the time and effort (and money) and it made me feel good. I felt appreciated, sought after, and began to let my guard down and just enjoy being pursued and the feelings that came with it, before I knew it, I fell in love with you.

Time passed and stressors began to pile up and I found myself having to step into the supportive and catering and fighting role. I began to pursue you for your attention and your heart and be the strength that you needed to get through your tough times, knowing all along I had no control on those things and just had to sit and hope you would recognize my efforts and appreciate them. You recognized my efforts but quickly forgot to cater to me and my emotions too. I began to resent you for needing me so much and resent the things and people that were causing you so much pain, that were making you take your focus off of me as a vulnerable and delicate part of your life and instead valuing/needing only my strength. Don't get me wrong, I believe both of us need to give both strength and vulnerability to each other but not one without the other. But I feel betrayed in the fact that my emotions got pushed so far aside and when the time rose for you to love and cherish and nurture my heart and delicacy (my beauty), you turned and ran. I quickly went back to feeling lonely and confused as to why I would be pushed away, why I wouldn't be chased after. I thought I was quite a catch and you had shown me in the beginning that you thought so too, but your actions and words spoke so strongly otherwise. "I don't want to work to get you back" still pierces my heart just as strongly today as it did a month or so ago. I'm scared I will never forget those words, because I was making myself vulnerable but still trying to be strong. They cut me deeper than anything I've ever been told. My desire was to find strength in you, in stepping up and offering your love to me when I needed you the most, I needed to feel special and beautiful by you again, after you had cut me down with your actions and words based off of fear.

Our relationship had so many signs of failure from our different backgrounds and lifestyles. I was ready to fight those battles with you, because I knew you were special and what we had was special. But fear of failure caused you to turn and run many times. I feel abandon by you and my hearts' desires are starved by your unwillingness to fight for me and for us. It wasn't going to be easy but I wanted to love and support us, support you in leading us towards our potential, to be my hero and the hero of our love story. I feel rejected by you because you gave way to the fear of failure. My heart and vulnerability are now wounded and the hardening process has begun again.

I truly don't know where I stand in my desires of us in the future, or if I really want or see a future with you. My ego, heart, and most importantly my trust are wounded. I don't know the next steps to take, or what it would take for me to start believing anything you said to me. I know after I let your last long text sink in, I wept. That is all I ever wanted to hear from you and to finally hear it from you, it began to wake my heart's desires again. I am going to go talk to someone soon myself, to help me sort out the jumble of emotions I feel about you and our situation, because I am anything but clear on it. I wanted to write this to you to break the silence I have had, and let you into my thoughts and feelings a little bit. But I should also say this isn't a "let's open the communication lines and work it out". I am still very unsure about things but this is a brief (maybe not so brief) explanation of my emotions and open wounds I have finally started to put into words. I do want to believe that you are making strides to better yourself as a man, and I am proud of you for that. I do miss you daily, and not a day goes by where I am not reminded of you in some form or fashion or think it would be nice to experience whatever with you on that particular day. I am trying so hard to cope and grieve the loss of you, so that I can begin the think clearly again as to what my heart truly wants.

*   *   *   *

Strength and stability is what the feminine heart desires and trust vaporizes then manifests in many ways toward the men who are supposed to bring both and fail them. Our society has taken the emphasis off male chivalry due to many forces.

However, is chivalry dead in our society? Let's think about two historical ship wrecks to see where we are. When the Titanic sank the cry was "women and children first" to get into the life rafts and many men waved goodbye to their families, knowing that the ship was sinking and they would never see them again. Fast forward to the cruise ship Costa Concordia that was not even out at sea but it was "every man (woman and child) for himself!" Real men need to halt this trend and make a statement to the world. All Pro Dad published a post *10 Acts a Chivalrous Husband Does for His Wife* and shared this summary.

> When a man opens the car door for his wife, he is doing far more than just getting the door open. It is not a matter of utility. It is not a question of pragmatics. Granted, we could save energy all around if both individuals opened their own doors. But he is making a statement in addition to getting the door open. He is disciplining his own heart and soul, which need it, and he is honoring his wife, who is glorified by it. The role of the man here, if we may speak this way, is not just to get the door open. His central role is the liturgical act of saying that women everywhere should be held in honor by men, and that he adds his amen to this, as everyone in the parking lot at Costco can now see.[17]

When was the last time you opened the door for your wife or a woman?!

But what does fighting for your woman look like? It can come on many fronts but it could be having patience with her as she struggles with insecurities. Your free time could be spent with her and the family instead of doing what you want to.

> The number one thing women tell me in counseling they want from their husbands – pray with them.
> ~ Mark Bagwell

You can be very intentional about being home emotionally and spiritually instead of just physically. You can honor her with your words. And most of all, you can be faithful to her with your eyes and thoughts. It looks different for all of us, but remember that your wife forsakes her individual freedom in clinging to you, believing you will provide love and strength. Your wife is still God's little ewe lamb, regardless of the pain and sin she's been through and the character wounds she carries. Don't forget: God has entrusted her to you. Will you resent her, or help her? Does your heart warm to the task of restoration? Is there any nobler act than pouring out your mercy on your precious one? Deal with your spouse based upon who she is today, not upon what you want her to be. So what if she isn't who she should be today? Are you? Besides, it's not important that she becomes everything you expect. It's important that she becomes like Christ. Your mercy and strength help carry her there."[18]

I have asked my now son-in-law John to share his masculine journey back as he came to an understanding of his masculine strength. I am so proud of him and honored to call him my son!

*   *   *   *

When I first met Tim in the winter of 2014, I had been dating his daughter, Olivia, for a couple months. On the outside, I thought things were going great. We were in a long distance relationship, Olivia in Nashville, TN and myself in a Boston, MA suburb. I was looking forward to meeting Tim and the rest of the family as one of the main things that brought Olivia and me together was our love for our families. As one can imagine, life was a little different for the two of us growing up. One of us right outside of Boston and one in the "deep south" of South Carolina. But our values we grew up with and the roots were very similar.

The first trip to Fair Play, SC to meet the Mays family was great. I finally had some young siblings around to play games with and enjoy the weekend with. Growing up, I had 5 brothers and sisters, however, they ranged from 10-20 years older than I was. When I was a kid, it was more so like they were extra parents. My parents themselves, were 44 and 45 when they had me so as I grew and was transitioning from a college student to a young man, it was sometimes tough to speak and have them relate with me. Needless to say, I felt right at home with Olivia's family. I can deal with a smaller family, and as mentioned it was nice to have some of her siblings around my age.

As I previously mentioned, on the outside, things seemed to be great. However, shortly after this trip, things started to crumble a bit for me. I was living at home and my father had Parkinson's disease and still battled with cancer, which he had years before and had just been maintaining it since. I was beginning to see him in a way that was just becoming hard to handle. As most kids see their dads, he was superman to me growing up. He was a strict father for sure, but I never once thought he didn't love me and would not do anything in his power to protect me, and to help push me to be the man I need to be. Because of this, when I would see him break down in tears because he felt useless —mostly for my mother—it ruined me. It was a hard time at that point with my parents and I tried to be their rock. I remember constantly hugging them both and saying "God won't give you more than you can handle." Funny enough, as I was telling them this, I'm not sure I felt that myself.

Another thing to mention about my current living situation was one of my older brothers was living at home as well. My brother is about 15 years older than me, had been married with a daughter, but was living back home after a tough divorce and substance abuse issues. One night, when my whole family was in Vermont (brother and parents) I went to an engagement party for one of my friends. His father was a local detective and asked me if I had a brother or father by my brother's name because they had tagged someone who had been pawning jewelry. This really was a gut punch. To be honest, after this whole situation was addressed, not much was done. My parents didn't know how to deal with my brother's addiction, as they were old school. You don't do drugs because it's wrong and it screws up your life is how they think of it. Plain and simple. But they were cautious as they were embarrassed and they didn't want to lose visiting right for their granddaughter.

One of my first weekends with Olivia I spoke about my situation with my brother and basically how we live in the same house, but I don't even talk to him. I didn't address it, I just had so much anger towards him for what he was doing to my parents, when they were dealing with their own issues. Of course, Olivia immediately realized that probably was not a good thing. And in May after I had met Tim, my world essentially crashed.

I broke down emotionally. I felt like I could not deal with everything going on around me. I wanted to be the rock for my parents and I wanted to help my brother get better. I wasn't doing either. Of course, there is nothing to do for Parkinson's but at the time my mind just was not comprehending that. And you also can't change someone with substance abuse to immediately heal them, which I wanted. I couldn't carry the weight anymore and through it all, I called Olivia and I told her I just can never move away from my family and I don't know if we should date.

After pushing Olivia away a couple times and having her tell me there will be no contact, I fell into a hard depression. Honestly, thinking back on it now, I can't comprehend ever feeling that way again. I would wake up, go to work, come home and get in bed. I was barely eating and I was losing weight. I love being social, love seeing my friends, and love being with people and having fun. I became the opposite and I didn't know what to do. I started losing a little faith to be honest as well. "Why was I going through all of this? Why did I have to deal with this? I was also thinking, am I going to turn into this brother who has the substance abuse?" My other two brothers are extremely successful men with great jobs and families. I admired them and still do. I had always said my three main role models were my dad and those brothers. But I was starting to doubt myself. I felt like I failed and I was only going to continue down that road.

Eventually, I reached out to Tim. Not to speak about Olivia, who wasn't talking to me at the time, but to just talk about what I was dealing with. I remembered how Olivia would speak so highly about Tim and how he has helped many people and I took a shot. I'd be lying if I wasn't skeptical, but I needed to speak with someone who wasn't right in the mix. I told Tim everything I felt. He started by telling me to talk to my two brothers, tell them how I look up to them, and make a point to just spend more time with my Dad because that is really all I could do.

Immediately we spoke about my relationship with Jesus. And as I mentioned before I was fading away at that point in time. Tim suggested a book to read and said he would send it up to me. A few days later, I received *Wild at Heart* by John Eldredge in the mail. There wasn't just a note from Tim, but also one from Alex, his son in-law. I was encouraged immediately to know I had these two behind me in my quest to move forward and be stronger. The plan was to read through and follow up with Tim every so often to discuss.

As I started reading, there was a lot I was looking for answers to. "How do I deal with my home life? And how can I work on myself, make myself better and stronger, in the case that Olivia does give me another chance?" It became clear to me I was in a very important part of my life. It was time to grow up and change from being a boy to being a man. I was really hurting over not having Olivia during the time, but starting to realize, I can never be what I need to be for her, if I don't fix myself on my own now. In the book, Eldredge wrote that "the masculine takes a man away from the woman so that he might return to her. He goes to find his strength; he returns to offer it." This really allowed me to put my faith in God and start focusing solely on me. And to be honest, I always saw that as somewhat selfish. Thinking about yourself, but I couldn't have been more wrong.

"Deep in his heart, every man long for a battle to fight, and adventure to live, and a beauty to rescue." These were the three things man needed in life Eldredge wrote. I started thinking into that. "What is my battle, what is my adventure, who was my beauty? I put the beauty aspect on the back burner, as it was clear I wanted to rescue Olivia. What was my battle and what was my adventure?" I felt as though I was in the battle at that time. I could make some changes personally or I could continue to live the life I was living and not battling my current state of mind. That is where I started.

I started focusing on things I could change. I would go to group meetings of family members with drug addiction to try to help myself. Tim put me in touch with a good friend of his who had battled his own addictions, so I could speak with him and talk through things on his end. In essence, I started worrying about my well-being over my brother's, knowing that it will be his choice when he wants to make that change. That was hard for me. I felt selfish and I felt like I was turning my back on blood. I felt bad because I didn't want to upset my parents, I didn't want them to think I didn't want to help my brother. I just couldn't and I needed to focus on myself. Slowly, things started to change. I was feeling a little better. I was realizing that I wasn't being selfish simply by putting my needs ahead of my brother's. I continued to tell him I will be here to support you if you wish but if you don't make changes there is nothing I can do.

I also started dealing with the battle I had in regards to my father's health. "Every boy, in his journey to become a man, takes an arrow in the center of his heart, in the place of his strength. Because the wound is rarely discussed and even more rarely healed, every man carries a wound." My Dad, my superman, was falling. And it felt exactly like a dagger. The other part that really affected me was that I was only 23 years old. I haven't had that much time with my father. I also realized that I missed an important time in his fatherhood. By the time I came around he was in older stages of his life. He was easy on me compared to my siblings for sure. I love my relationship with him and he always did and still does everything he can, but I missed about 20 years of his fatherhood. And there is almost a missed generation between the two of us. Once again, I was able to speak with Tim about this and relate, because he grew up in a similar family dimension, being the youngest by some time and an older father.

I made a point to spend more time with him. To speak to him in more depth. And to ask him questions about his youth, his pursuit of my mother, his time in the military, his time as a kid. I loved these stories as we just would sit and speak. We both are high on "quality time" as a love language and we started spending more together. This is not to say it didn't hurt me when I would see him struggle to do little things. I just learned that I needed to address it. Whether it was talking it out with Tim or just praying. His mind was fully intact and I would thank God every day for that aspect. So I continued my battle in learning how to deal with these scenarios and how to not let them hold me down. As I had always told my parents "God will only give you what you can handle." I actually started to think that way myself for once. Eldredge says "You can't fight a battle you don't know exists", and I was finally aware and attacking these battles.

Real Men

As I started focusing on adventure, I started thinking of my relationship with Olivia. She was my adventure. The long-distance relationship, the fact that to be together long-term I would probably have to leave my "safe boat." My whole family lived within 10-20 minutes of each other and I was the youngest of 6, in love with a girl living in Nashville, from South Carolina. It was definitely an adventure. She was my beauty to rescue and I knew that. I just needed to continue to work on myself until I got that chance. In *Wild at Heart* Eldredge also examines that men only pick battles they are sure to win. This was not one I was sure to win. And to be honest, it is partially the reason I pushed her away. I was completely different than a "good ole boy" of the south. I was often brash, I didn't look like a frat boy, and I was a northern Catholic, Italian boy. I was truly worried that I wouldn't be good enough. It was the epitome of a battle I didn't know if I could win.

I also didn't know if I could move south. But after months of working on myself, reading *Wild at Heart*, working on my relationship with God, and using Tim as a mentor, I felt I was moving in the right direction. I was starting to feel like myself again. I was more comfortable with my brother and to be honest, blunter with him during his battle. I was more comfortable with my parents and what they were going through. I actually felt more of a rock for them. And then came the email from Olivia.

She finally reached back out and laid everything out there. I knew I hurt her, and I knew it was going to take some time to get things back to good graces. She gave me that beauty to rescue. I knew this was my last chance. She opened up and told me things I had no idea about. Wounds she had that I never would have guessed. And there it was. My beauty.

It was late August and I went back to Nashville to see her for the first time since everything had happened. I was so scared and nervous. But I knew this was my chance. We enjoyed the weekend together and planned to continue moving forward. After a week later, I called and told her, I am ready to start planning a move to Nashville. This was my chance. Was it quick after we just started talking again? Sure. But it was my adventure. I had it in my head that if I move to Nashville and things don't work out, I'll spend a year in Nashville, a great city, and then figure it out from there. I was young enough that it wouldn't kill me. A few months later, we were planning my move.

When I was going through all my issues and feeling down about myself, I mentioned I started falling away from God and losing any relationship. I believe in his book, *Killing Lions*, Eldredge mentioned that when you say "Why God?" you need to realize it isn't God, but actually the devil disguised as God. I thought things were going great before everything happened. It was a façade. And the devil found his chance to swoop in and move me certain ways. This helped me realize that even when I thought things were going well, I need to always have my guard up because that is when he strikes quickest.

My move to Nashville wasn't perfect. I left my job I loved in Massachusetts and made the move south. Less than three months into my life in Nashville, I lost my job. Perfect time for me to fall back, but due to the new strength in my relationship with God and the ability to speak with someone such as Tim, I didn't let that ruin me. I actually found the positive from it. I moved somewhere, with no family, only Liv as my immediate support and I lost my job. I realized the support from Liv was all I needed and that things were going to be okay. I kept my faith and losing that job actually forced me to change careers. And I'm currently working in a position that I could not be happier with.

When I first met Tim and started my relationship with him, I was truly in a crossroads. Looking back, I was just moving through the motions, missing the college life, hating that I had to deal with real world issues with my family. It almost broke me. One of the best decisions I have made in life was to reach out directly to Tim even when I had no relationship with Olivia. It helped change my life. I say it all the time now, I can't imagine being in that state of depression I was in ever again. There is too much to be thankful for. I've been blessed with a loving family and am now lucky enough to call Tim my father-in-law and be a part of his family. I now have two more men to look up to and admire in regards to being a man and being a husband and father, Tim and my brother-in-law Alex.

* * * *

Your woman needs your masculine strength that is focused on the right thing and in the right way. When she feels safe, secure and wanted by you, she will respond. You make her feel like a princess, she will make you feel like a prince. The key is for each one to try to out give the other. When this happens, both get what they need and there are fireworks!

"William Wallace set the standard for sacrifice, bravery and courage showing us how to die, because he knew what he was living for."[19]

Love Languages

A small group that my wife and I were attending decided to do a study on *The Five Love Languages* by Gary Chapman. Understanding the concept changed my marriage after twenty-eight years! I highly recommend that you and your wife / girlfriend read the book together and talk about it or participate in a small group study with other couples. If you have children, profile them and apply the principles to your parenting techniques – it will change your world, and theirs! I am only going to hit the highlights so that you will get the basics and seek further study.

We all need and want to "feel loved", that we belong and are wanted. It is at the heart of our behavior as children and adults. Just as we are all unique, we have different love languages. In his years of counselling, Dr. Chapman narrowed them down to five major groupings. They are words of affirmation, quality time, receiving gifts, acts of service, and physical touch. Everyone has a "primary" and "secondary" language where we feel most loved when we are spoken to in it. Our primary love language is what we usually do when trying to communicate love to others. The "love tank" will determine how things go in that when full, life is good and when empty, not so good. A full tank brings out the best in us so if your children are misbehaving, think about their love language and tank level.

People get married when they are "in love" which will last about two years and then they have to choose to love the person they are married to. Think about the marriages that are in trouble after a couple of years. As the illusion of intimacy evaporates, individual desires, emotions, thoughts and behavior patterns appear and you realize that you are two individuals. It is at this point in many marriages that couples "fall out of love" and withdraw, separate, divorce and set off in a new in love experience. Those who want to make it, must begin the hard work of learning to love each other without the euphoria of the in-love obsession. [20]

This information was life-changing for me because it explained why I felt frustrated many times and, as you saw with the anger section, that frustration manifested as anger. I realized that Jill's language was acts of service and receiving gifts. I was filling her tank regularly doing things for her and giving her gifts all along. There were many times that I just needed a hug but had to initiate getting one if it was going to happen – not much movement in the tank gauge. I am a "toucher" and the more comfortable I am with someone, the more it comes out. In this day and time, I really have to keep my guard up on this. Knowing why I feel the way I do, helps me understand and not allow myself to become frustrated and come out as anger.

Another way that the concept helps is in parenting. Regrettably, our children were grown by the time I understood this but reflecting back it makes so much sense with a situation we had with our daughter Olivia. Children tend to gravitate to one parent, particularly when there are multiples. Abby had developed a closer relationship with Jill and Olivia to me. They each say that we love the other one more but we will revisit that when they have their own kids. Things were well in Olivia's world but then our son Chandler was born and things changed. We had not timed things ideally with Jill starting her nursing school clinicals and major studies when he was just seven months old. I took on the majority of the household duties while Jill dove into her school work. This pulled me out of Olivia's world as she knew it. Now, we realize that her language is quality time and there was none available from me and certainly not from Jill. This had a negative impact on Olivia that in hindsight could have been minimized if not eliminated had we known and applied the love language concept. I believe if I had carved out a weekly event for the two of us, her tank would have been filled and problems avoided. We have talked about this with Olivia and she agrees that it would have helped the situation. As parents, you just do the best you can with what you know. Please see what your family members' love languages are and learn how to speak them. All of the profiles can be accessed on line at 5lovelanguages.com I recently read something in a devotional that I receive that adds another dimension worth sharing regarding the communication of love and respect in marriage. Dr. Emerson

Eggerichs shared that women speak "love language" while men speak "respect language."[21] This struck a chord with me in that the times I feel disrespected I get angry. I think this might be a key concept with the domestic violence issue. If men will learn and speak love then women understand and implement speaking with respect, communication can happen. My son-in-law, Alex, once made a statement about a conflict he had gotten in with Abby's friend that rings true here. He said that "she does not have to respect me but I do not have to let her disrespect me." We have to get women to understand this truth about men and as men, we need to add this as a source of anger as we evaluate it. The book *Love and Respect* is another game changer no matter how long you have been married but particularly for about-to-be- or just-married couples.

Iron Sharpens Iron – having the right men in your life

One of the enemy's tools where men are concerned is the lie that you don't need anyone, and if you do you are weak. Because we do not want to appear weak or unmanly, we stay isolated thinking we are the only one struggling with insecurity, fear, or sexual sin. Remember that our greatest fear is being found out, so we don't let anyone in or close enough to us to see behind the mask. We all also want and need to feel loved, men included. While at a Radical Mentoring Summit, John Lynch, author of *On My Worst Day, Bo's Café,* and *The Cure* shared these concepts with the group. He stated that people (men) feel that "if you see the real me you would not love me, so I wear a mask so you will." The mask is worn because of weakness, failure, or limitations actually resulting in men never getting loved. But each of us were created with limitations so that we can be loved. Men need and desire a safe place where "the worst of you" can be loved. In that place, we can take off our masks and admit areas in our lives that are not going well and draw on other men to walk through it with us.

Ideally, there is a place where we can admit the sin that we are intending to commit. When we can share what we have done, or are thinking of doing, the power of sin is broken. Otherwise, unresolved sin is buried alive and is revived as a tool of the enemy to keep us "on the shelf" feeling unable to serve God. The Bible tells us to *confess your sins one to another* but that should occur in a safe place with those who you trust and who trust you. We need a safe place to fail and to allow ourselves to be vulnerable. Lynch further explained that "transparency" is when we let someone know what's going on with us, often for our own purpose. "Vulnerability" on the other hand, is when we give someone the bullets to shoot us with. "Vulnerability" has a reciprocal effect and is a by-product not a goal of the relationship.

We all need this "safe place" as men, but we are hesitant to pursue it or do not know where to find it. I encourage you to find that "Band of Brothers" who can do life with you and help you understand that you are not alone. My church has a saying that "it's OK not to be Ok, but it's not OK to stay there." We need other men in our lives who are going in the same direction, have been where we want to go and will be honest with us in a non-condemning way. We were all born on purpose, for a purpose, and with a purpose. The Bible tells us in Ephesians 3:20 that Jesus is *able to do immeasurably more than all we ask or imagine* but *the enemy comes to kill, steal and destroy* (John 10:10). Satan does not want you to become the man who God designed you to be. If he can keep you alone, he can stunt that process. We have to take an active role in the battle for our masculinity. One of our core principles at my church is "You can't do life alone." Don't let the Devil keep you isolated so that he can "pick you off" in your masculine journey. Find your safe place.

Once experienced, having a group of men who you feel you can be honest with is addictive. We really need other men in order to become the men we were designed to be. Morgan Snyder with Ransomed Heart Ministries shared this concept in his blog *Who Will Carry Your Casket?*

> Being a groomsman says, "I will." Carrying a casket says, "I did." The masculine journey is a time of being refined by fire. Broken down. Built up. Repeat the process.
> Jesus suggests that the gate and the road are wide that lead to death and many choose to travel that path. The path to life, which few choose, is one with a narrow gate and a narrow road. I want to find it. I want you to as well. And entering through the narrow gate and traveling the narrow road is a journey that cannot be done alone.
> In this decade of excavation and becoming good soil, I've

come to define a peer as "someone who wants the same thing I want and has to fight through the same crap to get it."

Find like-hearted kings living in the same direction. Sign treaties. When one kingdom is at war, both are at war. On how many fronts can you successfully fight a war and be victorious? Be honest. And for how much of your time in any given day/week/year can you be at war and still sustain life over the long term? It will only be a few. And it's always been that way: Jesus offers the model with his closest brothers-in-arms.

We cannot live a supernatural life and travel the narrow road without signing a few treaties with a select few good and holy kings. Who will carry your casket? What stories will they tell of the camaraderie you shared in both the thrill of victory and the agony of defeat? Solomon says that a man is worse off than a stillborn child if he does not receive a proper burial (Ecclesiastes). I can imagine few things more central to a proper burial than who will carry my casket. It will only be a few. Ask God to speak their names.[22]

I recently was introduced to a word that captures what every man needs in his life, at least one. *Cymbrogi* (koom-BRO-gee) is a Celtic term for "sword brothers." A sword brother is one who has covenanted to stand with his comrade in battle for noble causes and who would gladly forfeit his life for his brother in arms. Jesus said, *Greater love has no one than this: to lay down one's life for one's friends.* John 15:13 NIV. We need godly men in our lives who will guard our souls. Manhood is a battle that has to be fought for and cannot be done alone.

Two are better than one, because they have a good reward for their labor. For if they fall, one will lift up his companion. But woe to him who is alone when he falls, for he has no one to help him up. Again, if two lie down together, they will keep warm; but how can one be warm alone? Though one may be overpowered by another, two can withstand him. And a threefold cord is not quickly broken. Ecclesiastes 4:9-12 NKJV.

What Cha Gonna Do with This?

We need Real Men! Families need them, churches need them, and our communities need them. Your journey to becoming a "real man" starts by understanding that I am here for a reason; I have the strength to fulfill it; I have to discover it and direct it in a positive way. You can start right now, because it is never too late to do the right thing.

Once you decide the man you want to be, your choices are really made for you. You simply ask "Can I do that or not do that and be the man I have decided to be?" Some will not know how to handle a real man but if you have ever been in the company of one, you can feel his presence. Eldredge tells us in *Wild at Heart*, "Let people feel the weight of who you are and let them deal with it."[23]

So how do you want your life to be remembered? One of my favorite poems is by Linda Ellis, *The Dash*

> I read of a man who stood to speak at the funeral of a friend.
> He referred to the dates on her tombstone from the beginning to the end.
> He noted that first came the date of her birth and spoke of the following date with tears.
> But he said what mattered most of all was the dash between those years.
> For that dash represents all the time that she spent alive on earth
> and now only those who loved her know what that little line is worth.
> For it matters not, how much we own, the cars, the house, the cash,
> what matters is how we live and love and how we spend our dash.
> So think about this long and hard; are there things you'd like to change?
> For you never know how much time is left that can still be rearranged.
> If we could just slow down enough to consider what's true and real
> and always try to understand the way other people

feel.
And be less quick to anger
And show appreciation more
And love the people in our lives like we've never loved before.
If we treat each other with respect and more often wear a smile, remembering that this special dash might only last a little while.
So when your eulogy is being read with your life's actions to rehash,
Would you be proud of the things they say about how you spent your dash?

James tells us, *You don't know the first thing about tomorrow. You're nothing but a wisp of fog, catching a brief bit of sun before disappearing.* James 4:14 MSG

Jesus said, *lay up for yourselves treasures in heaven, where neither moth nor rust destroys and where thieves do not break in and steal.* Matthew 6:20 NKJV

We are not promised tomorrow, only today. So are you going to make it count? All Pro Dad publishes a *Play of the Day* that contains some good material for being a good dad. One of the publications contained *5 Things You Want Said about You at Your Funeral* outlining noble statements made at a man's eulogy.

1. This world is a better place because he lived!
2. He knew what was important in life!
3. This was a faithful man.
4. His family is going to miss him…but he left them equipped to thrive.
5. He lived to the full, and he didn't waste the gift of life!

How about you? The key is that we have to spend our lives doing the things that will produce these statements when our days on this earth are over.[24]

I heard about a young bride, Paige Eding, who stopped at her Daddy's grave on the way to her wedding. It hit me hard that you never know how long you have. I got to dance with my daughters but there are no guarantees in life, so make the best of the time you have.

I want to close this chapter with words copied off a wall at Fort Leavenworth, Kansas at the Tactical Commander's Development Course in the mid 90's are the words to consider as you step into the daily battle.

War is an ugly thing, but not the ugliest of things.
Uglier by far is the decayed and degraded state of moral and patriotic feeling that thinks nothing is worth war.
A man who has nothing for which he is willing to fight, nothing he values more than his own safety, is a miserable creature who has no chance of being free unless…made so and kept so through the exertions of better men than himself.

Those words were read at my Daddy's funeral. I hope they will encourage you to pursue your manhood and to be significant as a man. Taking this step will mean that you are stepping into battle.

Be a *Better Man*! Be a *Real Man*. The world needs you! This matters!

"Our greatest fear should not be of failure, but at succeeding at something that does not matter."
~ D.L. Moody

STEP 5 - UNDERSTAND THAT EVIL EXISTS AND MUST BE BATTLED DAILY

This is a Battleship not a Cruise Ship!

Warning! Once you have made a decision to enter into a relationship with Jesus Christ or get serious about making your relationship with Him stronger, you need to be aware of something that will happen. You now have a big target on your back. You are about to enter the battle of spiritual warfare that is fought primarily in your head. You will have thoughts of doubt, condemnation, and confusion about what you have just done.

There is someone who is NOT happy with your decision and his name is Lucifer.

Chip Ingram characterized our enemy and his tactics in his message series *The Invisible War* in his book by the same title. His other names tell us more about what his efforts are directed toward. He is "Satan", your adversary; the "Devil", slanderer; "Tempter"; and "Accuser of the brethren." His goal is to terrorize your soul; render you impotent as a believer; make you worthless to the cause of Christ or make your life one of misery and spiritual defeat.

Ingram established five basic truths about spiritual warfare we are in:

1. There is an invisible world that is just as real as the visible world.
2. We are involved in an invisible war, a cosmic conflict that has eternal implications.
3. Our foe is formidable and his goal is to destroy us and discredit the cause of Christ.
4. We must respect our foe, but not fear him – become acutely aware of his methods but not preoccupied by them.
5. As a believer in Christ we do not fight *for* victory, we fight *from* victory – in Christ's power we are invincible.[1]

Be alert and of sober mind. Your enemy, the devil, prowls around like a roaring lion, looking for someone to devour. 1 Peter 5:8 NIV

In his message series *Diabolical: Satan's Agenda for Planet Earth...including you*, Chip explains that a lion roars to create fear, it is stealth for attack because he is not going to let his prey know he is about to attack. A lion will roar for territorial protection; communication or to express anger.

He further cites two dangerous ways of thinking about the enemy. "Too much", in that everything that happens has to do with demons, or "too little", where nothing that happens has to do with demons. Most spiritual warfare happens in your head so your thought process is key in this cosmic battle.[2]

In *Wild at Heart*, Eldredge outlines the stages of his strategy. The Bible speaks of "schemes" which is a "game plan" for bringing you down. Just as in sports, the enemy looks for weaknesses or over-used strengths that can be capitalized upon to defeat the opponent.

The first stage is "I'm not here." If there is no enemy then there is no need to fight.

Once you understand the enemy and decide to take a stand he goes into action with open assaults, and your mind starts the games as he tries to "intimidate" you as his second stage. A thought will enter your mind and you will think "where did that come from?" Just remember that the Holy Spirit will "convict" you, and the devil will "condemn" you. Evaluate your thoughts!

If he is unsuccessful at the first two, he then moves to the third stage and tries to "cut a deal" with us.[3] We allow the conversations in our heads thinking that we deserve that pleasure, and it won't hurt just one time or no one will ever know. The next thing we know, we have stumbled and he has been successful in making us feel "unusable" by God – "shelved."

James explained the process this way,

When we are tempted, no one should say, God is tempting me. For God cannot be tempted by evil, nor does He tempt anyone; but each person is tempted when they are dragged away by their own evil desires and enticed. Then, after desire has conceived, it gives birth to sin; and sin, when it is full-grown, gives birth to death. 1:13-15 NIV.

Being tempted is not a sin but if we allow it to linger in our mind long enough, we act on it and fall into sin. This is what Jesus was talking about when He said *whoever looks at a woman lustfully has already committed adultery with her in his heart.* Matthew 5:28 NIV. We have to think about something before we do it. Understand the enemy and his tactics because he comes to *kill, steal and destroy* our lives. The only way to fight is to use the weapons that are available to us. Paul tells us in Ephesians 6:13-18 about the *armor of God* that we are to equip ourselves daily to fight the battle we are in. John Eldredge crafted a practical application of this passage in *Wild at Heart.*

> Therefore put on the full armor of God, so that when the day of evil comes, you may be able to stand your ground, and after you have done everything, to stand. Stand firm then, with the belt of truth buckled around your waist..."Lord, I put on the belt of truth. I choose a lifestyle of honesty and integrity. Show me the truths I so desperately need today. Expose the lies I'm not even aware that I'm believing." ...with the breastplate of righteousness in place ... "and yes, Lord, I wear your righteousness today against all condemnation and corruption. Fit me with your holiness and purity – defend me from all assaults against my heart." ... and with your feet fitted with the readiness that comes from the gospel of peace ... "I do choose to live for the gospel at any moment. Show me where the larger story is unfolding and keep me from being so lax that I think the most important thing today is the soap operas of this world." In addition to all this, take up the shield of faith, with which you can extinguish all the flaming arrows of the evil one ... "Jesus, I lift against every lie and every assault the confidence that You are good, and that you have good in store for me. Nothing is coming today that can overcome me because You are with me"....Take the helmet of salvation... "Thank you, Lord for my salvation. I receive it in a new and fresh way from You and I declare that nothing can separate me now from the love of Christ and the place I shall ever have in Your kingdom"....and the sword of the Spirit, which is the word of God... "Holy Spirit, show me specifically today the truths of the Word of God that I will need to counter the assaults and the snares of the Enemy. Bring them to mind throughout the day"....And pray in the Spirit on all occasions with all kinds of prayers and requests. With this in

mind, be alert and always keep praying for the saints. "Finally, Holy Spirit, I agree to walk in step with You in everything – in all prayer as my spirit communes with you throughout the day."[4]

Most of us get into trouble when we allow ourselves to be alone. *A man who isolates himself seeks his own desire; He rages against all wise judgment.* Proverbs 18:1 NKJV. This is when our chances of getting *picked off* are greatly increased. The lion does not attack the herd but the one that is out away and alone. Again, we need others in our lives who will encourage us and fight with us. We have the power and there is strength in numbers. *Submit yourselves, then, to God. Resist the devil, and he will flee from you.* James 4:7 NIV.

In his book, *Samson and the Pirate Monks*, Nate Larkin walks through his journey to understand that isolation is a man's greatest weakness in our fight for integrity.

> …my idea of integrity was unrealistic and unbiblical, and this basic understanding had prevented me from experiencing the power and sweetness of the gospel. I had been trying to be God rather than love God, trying to reach a place where I merited God's mercy and really didn't need it anymore. My ambitions had been way out of whack. Yes, it is true, he said that God wants men of integrity. But integrity is not perfection. It is not completion. It is not even purity of intention, something that, frankly, we are all incapable of achieving. Rather, integrity is a rigorous honesty about my own condition and humble faith in the steadfast love of God."[5] Nate further goes on to tell of how The Samson Society[6] came into existence for men to understand and avoid getting "picked off" by the enemy as Samson did because he was alone. Christianity is a team sport and men have to grasp the idea that you can't do life alone and live victorious.

Remember, As believers in Christ, we do not fight "for" victory, we fight "from" victory. In Christ's power we are invincible![7]

Satan is a defeated foe, and we need to remind him of that

every chance we get. We know we win, read the end of The Book, so let's run up the score! But we have to fight from the power of Jesus and not on our own strength and not alone.

The visual that helped me is that we are traveling on a ship, the course is set but our activity is ours to decide on the boat. Our life's journey is on a cruise ship or a battle ship. How we conduct ourselves is determined by which one we realize we are on.

Learn the Enemy and fight like a real man! The outcome has eternal implications.

If you know the enemy and know yourself, you need not fear the result of a hundred battles. If you know yourself but not the enemy, for every victory gained you will also suffer defeat. If you know neither the enemy nor yourself, you will succumb in every battle.
~ Sun Tzu The Art of War

Run Up the Score!

BE SOMEBODY AND DO SOMETHING

I now realize that the journey God set me on in 2011 started long before then. He had been preparing me and others for "such a time as this." The introduction to the book of Esther in the Maxwell Leadership Bible gives accurate words to what I have experienced in the ongoing journey I am on.

> Helping younger men find the peace, purpose and fulfillment of living God-centric lives gives me unparalleled peace, purpose and fulfillment in my life.
> ~ Regi Campbell

God always takes the initiative in executing His plan. Then he looks for a person who will submit to Him, makes that individual aware of a need, and the need quickly becomes the personal burden of the person God has chosen. Ultimately, the individual embraces God's plan and feels morally compelled to act on it. The vision becomes his or her possession. Finally, the person calls others to join the cause, often at great personal risk.[1] Explaining God's Providence, God sees beforehand and "orchestrates" events to accomplish His purposes.[2]

I have seen situations change and people enter my life at just the right time that coincided with my ability to receive it.

We all have the desire to do something with our lives. The title of the message that got my attention was, *Don't Waste Your Life*. As men get older and enter into the "second half" of our lives, we have to think, "Does my life really matter? and, when I am gone, is there a part of me that will live on?" Jesus told us to *store up treasures in heaven* and the only thing on this earth that will make it out is people. The only thing that will last on earth are the things that you pass on to other people and the positive difference you made in their lives. When you pour into the lives of other men and are about your Father's business of building His Kingdom, every now and then He may give you a glance into your treasure chest – I have coined it a "God-peek." I had the pleasure of leading my college roommate to the Lord years after we graduated. I was saved right out of college and Bryan did not finish school and went down the path of admitting alcoholism and recovering through Alcoholics Anonymous with "the higher power as he understood it." He went back to school and got his degree then moved on with a life of successful sobriety through self-effort and the twelve-step process. We stayed in touch and I tried to appropriately nudge him to "The Higher Power" when possible but with no success, in my opinion. This is a perfect example of where Paul explains that *some plant, some water and others reap but it is God Who gives the increase* (1 Corinthians 3:5-10). God was working in Bryan's life and when he was coming home to visit he asked me to get a bite to eat because he wanted to talk with me about something. He shared that while he was recruiting male mentors for an organization in Florida, he met with a group of Christian men who get together weekly to study the Bible and support each other. He said, "they have something that I know I don't have and I want it." Talk about shooting fish in a barrel! At a barbeque place in Central, South Carolina, I had the honor and pleasure of introducing Bryan to "The Higher Power" he had been searching for and reaching out to but had no relationship with. I have watched him grow in steps toward a faith that is developing in the right direction and pace for him. Fast forward to a group I meet with on Wednesdays that Bryan is now a part of and it was his time to lead. I saw with my eyes a little peek at part of my treasure in heaven as I heard how God had changed and is changing his life – and I got to have a little part in it! That's how it works, we each have a role to play in helping others meet and follow Jesus, one step at a time.

So we all have a "calling" to be a part of something bigger and advance the kingdom. Regi Campbell says that "Men feel a calling to give back. To build into other men. To pay it forward." He also goes on to say, "calling is connected to design" in that, we have this desire in us and at some point we begin to pay attention to it. We want to "be somebody and do something" by our designed purpose. ..."we want to share that knowledge and experience with others. Mentoring is simply that...sharing what we've learned about living life with guys who are a few steps behind us on the path." [3]

Caution!

Before you take off to scratch that itch, let me share a few lessons that I have learned along my journey.

Be sure of your motive. You can do the right thing for the wrong reason. Regi Campbell says that "great mentors have made sense of their lives. You can't help someone else make sense of their life until you've made sense of your own."[4] So spend some time making sense of what God has been trying to teach you about it. Read books and let it sink in and talk with someone more spiritually mature than you that will speak truth in love. The best one to start with is definitely *Wild at Heart* by John Eldredge as you can see by how frequently I have referenced it. The other one I highly recommend to help figure things out is *Experiencing God* by Henry and Richard Blackaby along with Claude King. God used this book to help me realize that while I was doing some good things, it was too much about me and "doing" instead of "becoming."

Don't be in a hurry to be constantly engaged in activities for God. He may spend years preparing your character or developing your love relationship with Him before He gives you a large assignment...God will first build some basic foundations into your life before He gives you a larger role in service to Him.[5]

The relationship is what it is all about with God and not what you do or don't do, thinking He will love you more. ..."the goal of God's activity in your life - that you come to know Him...Don't bypass the relationship...Don't try to skip over the relationship to get on with the activity."[6] "We may accomplish our objectives but forego the relationship. It is possible to achieve all of our goals and yet be outside God's will...The world claims results are important; God values people...When we do the work of God in our own strength and wisdom, we will never see the power of God in what we do. We will only see what we can do through our own creativity and hard work...Every time we minister to people in our strength rather than God's power, people lose out."[7] Boy did this speak volumes to me!

God continued to speak to me through other writings as well.

Right motives can be illusive. One minute you can be pure in why you do what you do, the next you can subtly slip into suspect behavior. Therefore, be relentless to regularly review your motives. Pride is always looking to pounce on your purposes, so ask the Lord to cleanse your motives and mark them with His purposes. You can make faith in Jesus a filter for right motives. "Why would Jesus do this?" is a wise question that helps you get to the heart of the matter. The why question reveals intent and encourages honesty....your misguided motives will cause others discomfort, for they have a ripple effect on relationships and organizational dynamics. Unhealthy motives that seek attention and credit will compromise principles and values in an effort to reach the desired results. It is driven by whatever means necessary to justify worthy results, but lasting fruit results from the seeds of pure motives. Right motives reap God's rewards."[8]

I use the Maxwell Leadership Bible for my quiet time, I highly recommend it, and about the time God was speaking into my life on this subject I was reading in the book of Judges and found these nuggets of wisdom.

Self-promotion may 'work' in the short run, but over the long-haul God makes sure that it fails. *Humble yourselves, therefore, under God's mighty hand, that he may lift you up in due time.* (1 Peter 5:6) NIV[9]

I have learned much about "humility" and "due time" realizing that it is a process that God has been and continues taking me to fulfill His purpose in me. I am not there yet, but I know that it is coming and have become more content in my journey. In the process of due time, God provides time to 1) Cultivate a vision for my life, 2) Make my purpose clear, and 3) Give me confidence.[10] So don't be in a hurry. Allow God to prepare you. This is hard for men because our pride gets in the way. Pride is at the root of all evil and is what brought Lucifer down then Adam and Eve. I have recently recognized that I am prideful and it has been the source of many bad choices and damaged relationships. The Bible speaks so much about "humility" and how it is the way to be like Christ. Humility is "teachableness" and we have to figure out that we don't know everything before we can learn something. God can work with you when you get to that point – for some, like me, it takes a little longer to get there. I think I have finally turned the corner! But remember that humility is not weakness but controlled strength. If we just think of others like we do ourselves, our decisions and actions will follow. Be careful about pride, and don't let it be your motive for mentoring others.

Looking for love in all the wrong places

I recently ran across an illustration that summed up the things that I have learned since setting out on my journey to help ReBuild Real Men. We are all searching for something, and it is a process to realize it and then move through the steps of dealing with it.

Our church series leading up to Christmas focused on the people of the Christmas story. The message on the wise men particularly shined a new light on the representation of the gifts related to the search everyone has. The gold is for royalty in that we all want to follow someone and be part of something bigger than ourselves, God. The frankincense is a priestly tool and reminds us that we know we need help with our access to God. Finally, the myrrh meant the sacrifice because we know deep down that we are not "good enough" and there has to be a price paid. Therefore, our purpose in mentoring other males is to help them recognize their search and realize that all of the stuff in their lives has detoured them down many unhealthy avenues to find what they are looking for. A relationship, new or improved, with God has to be our purpose for everything we do or it will not last – no treasure.

Our fundamental needs as humans are a sense of worth and if it is missing, we feel inferior. Then we need a sense of belonging because if it is missing, we feel insecure. Another need is a sense of purpose so that we do not feel illegitimate. Finally, we need a sense of competence because if it is missing, we feel inadequate.[11] When we have these present in our lives, we feel secure. But this situation does not exist as a human being.

Insecurity drives what we think and what we do. Common symptoms of feeling insecure are when we compare ourselves with others and keep score. Or we may feel like a victim and must be compensated for our losses. Another symptom is to become self-consumed and try to outdo others for attention. Being driven to perform in order to gain others' approval is a sign of insecurity. When we judge others or ourselves, resulting in self-pity or conceit, is a sign of being insecure. And finally, when we must take charge, protect our interests and manipulate, insecurity is the source. Well that about sums it up for just about everyone! We are all insecure in one, multiple, or all areas of our lives. A key to overcoming it is recognizing it and seeking to do something about it.

To reduce personal insecurities in your life the first step is to establish your identity, *not your performance*, in Chris. Then allow God to break you of self-sufficiency and self-promotion. Third is to discover and practice your God-given purpose in life, not someone else's. Finally, learn to affirm others and receive affirmation.[12]

All of this is a process of "recognizing and reconciling" – mentoring is the means to help it start and come about.

The graphic below is taken from Tim Elmore's book *Lifegiving Mentors*[13] and I have added the sources I have discovered along my journey.

The root and fruit of our behavior

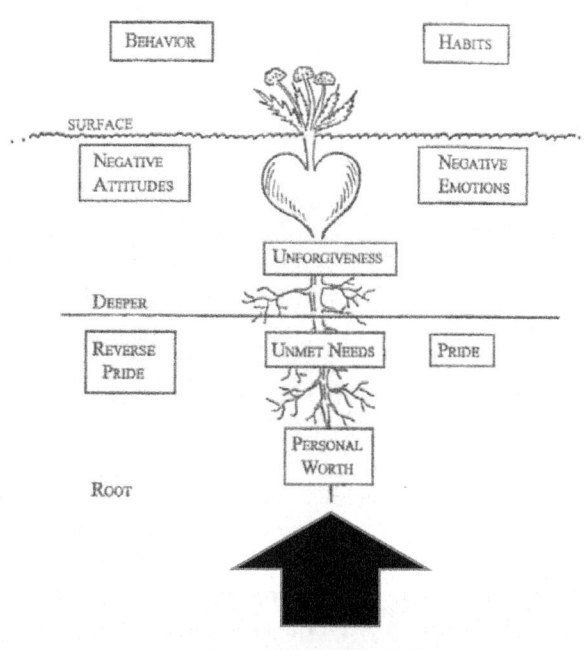

- BEHAVIOR
- HABITS
- SURFACE
- NEGATIVE ATTITUDES
- NEGATIVE EMOTIONS
- UNFORGIVENESS
- DEEPER
- REVERSE PRIDE
- UNMET NEEDS
- PRIDE
- PERSONAL WORTH
- ROOT

Verbal and/or Sexual Abuse
Divorce / Abandonment
Birth Order
Boundaries
Mother Relationship
Father Relationship

Childhood

Most, if not all, males are "unfathered" in a few or in all areas, but the outcome is the same – insecurity which leads to bad behavior and habits which lead to most if not all of our social ills. I do believe that if men would understand and assume their God-given roles, our nation and world would be a better place. The only way for them to get there is for older men to make sense of their lives and then "father" the younger ones in making sense of theirs.

Elmore describes this as the lack of the blessing. We all need the blessing which consists of a meaningful touch; the spoken word; expression of high value in us; a description of a special future; and a genuine commitment to our success that should come from our father as we grow up in a healthy environment.[14] The following excerpt is from John Eldredge's book *Fathered by God* that shows what being "fathered" looks like.

Fathered on the South Platte

I moved to Colorado in August of 1991. There were many reasons involved in the move from Los Angeles – a job, a shot at grad school, an escape form the seemingly endless asphalt-smog-and-strip-mall suffocation of L.A. – but beneath them all was a strong desire to get to the mountains and the wide-open spaces, get within reach of wildness. I couldn't have articulated it at the time, but my soul was yearning to take up the masculine journey that felt aborted in my early teens. And with that, I wanted to become a fly fisherman.

My dad and I fished together when I was young, and those are among my most treasured memories of him. He taught me first to fish with a worm on a bobber, and then cast a spinning rod. He was not a fly fisherman, but I wanted to be. Around the age of twenty-five, I bought myself a rod and reel and began to try to teach myself – a pattern by which, unfortunately, I have learned most of what I've learned in my life. We often speak of a man who's done this successfully as a *self-made man*. The appellation is usually spoken with a sense of admiration, but really it could be said in the same tones we might use of the dearly departed, or a man who recently lost an arm – with sadness yet regret. What the term really means is "an orphaned man who figured how to master some part of life on his own."

Back to fly-fishing. When we got to Colorado I learned of a section of the South Platte River known for its reputation as a fly fisherman's dream. The *Miracle Mile* was past its heyday, but still a place that the best fly fishermen headed to, and so I went. It's a beautiful stretch of river that flows through open ranchland between two reservoirs. The banks are low and spacious, with only the occasional willow – a forgiving place for a novice to learn to cast. I spent the good part of a morning in the river, seeing trout all around me but unable to catch one. Every time I looked upriver there was this guy, rod bent double, laughing and whooping as he brought yet another giant rainbow to his net. At first I envied him. Then I began to hate him. Finally, I chose humility and simply wanted to watch him for a while, try to learn what he was doing.

I stood at a respectful distance up the bank, not wanting to appear as an encroacher on his beloved spot, and sat down to watch. He was aware of me, and after casting maybe two or three times and hooking yet another fish, he turned and said, "C'mon down." I forget his name, but he told me he was a fly-fishing guide by profession, and on his days off this was where he most liked to fish. He asked me how I was doing and I said, "Not so good." "Lemme see your rig." I handed him my rod. "Oh...well, first off, your leader isn't long enough." Before I could apologize for being a fishing idiot, he had taken out a pair of clippers and nipped off my leader completely. He then tied on a new leader with such speed and grace I was speechless. "What flies you been usin'?" "These" I said sheepishly, knowing already they were the wrong flies only because I figured everything I was doing was wrong.

Graciously he made no comment on my flies, only said, "Here – this time of year you want to use these", pulling a few small midges off his vest and handed them to me. He tied one on my tippet, and then began to show me how to fish his treasured spot. "C'mon over here, right next to me." If a fly fisherman is right-handed, the instructor typically stands close on his left so as not to take the forward cast in the ear or back of his head. "Now – most folks use one strike indicator when they're fishing the fly below the surface [I felt good that at least I knew that – had read it in a book]. "But that won't help you much. You've got to know you you're getting a dead drift." Success in fly-fishing rests upon many nuances, but chief among them is your ability to present your fly naturally to the fish which means that it drifts down with the current in the same fashion as the real food they see every day – without tugging or pulling motion contrary to the speed and direction of the current. "The secret is to use two, even three. Like this." After about ten minutes of coaching, he stepped out of the water to watch me – just as a father who's taught his son to hit a baseball steps back to watch, let the boy take a few swings all by himself. I hooked a trout and landed it. He came back into the water to show me how to release it. "I usually kiss mine on the forehead. Superstition." He laid one on the brow of the large rainbow and released it into the cold water. "Have fun", he said, and without looking back he went downriver about to the spot where I'd been fishing earlier and began to catch fish there, one after another. I caught fish too. And while that made me happy, there was a deeper satisfaction in my soul as I stood in the river, fishing well. Some primal need had just been touched and touched good. As I drove home I know the gift had been from God, that He had fathered me through this man.[15]

Peeing on the electric fence

Emotional and even physical poverty stems from broken relationships, beginning with our relationship with God, then others around us in creation.[16] Therefore, our efforts in mentoring should focus on helping people recognize their broken relationships and the impact. However, if the relationship with their Heavenly Father is not reconciled first, other relationships will not be restored to the full potential.

> There are three kinds of men.
> The ones that learn by reading.
> The few that learn by observation.
> The rest of them have to pee on the electric fence for themselves.
> ~ Will Rogers

Change is hard for all of us, particularly with things hidden for years and one may not even be aware of their existence. Change begins when something triggers the individual to reflect upon his current situation and to think about a possible future situation that they prefer. Then he must decide to do something about it and take action upon the decision.[17] A man may not be ready to make a change so that is why mentoring needs to be strategic and with someone who wants to have an "opportunity" to make a better choice in his life-decisions. I have heard it referred to as "being sick and tired of being sick and tired." The role of the mentor is simply to show him what it looks like and how we got there.

Who's your Daddy?

As you consider entering into this fathering role, remember that it is to show males how things work based on the lessons you have learned. Nate Larkin described this well in his book.

Because no human parent is perfect, every one of us is wounded during childhood, whether we recognize it or not. In ways big and small, the injuries inflicted by our parents impair our vision and restrict our movement, and our reactions against them produce all kinds of self-sabotaging impulses. Most of us start noticing our parents' imperfections during adolescence, and soon we are seeking surrogates among our peers or in popular culture. We may also look for that perfect teacher or perfect boss, an all-wise and all-caring adult who can explain the universe and show us our place in it. On some level, we're all looking for Pop.

But in the end, every one of our replacement parents disappoints us, because no human parent is perfect. Eventually we may decide to tackle the job on our own, to 'parent ourselves,' and we may try to salve the pain of our childhood by becoming a parent to others. If we have any aptitude for the role, it's fairly easy for us to attract disciples. Lots of people are looking for a surrogate parent. Inevitably, however, we disappoint all our followers to some degree. As our faults begin to show, our disillusioned disciples may drift away in search of better parents, revert to orphan status, or decide it's time to assume the parental role themselves.

Jesus always said that He lived His life in full view of heaven, constantly conscious of His Father's gaze, trusting His care and seeking only to do His will. Jesus taught His disciples to pray to 'Our Father Who is in heaven,' and to trust their heavenly Father to meet their daily needs. He promised that after His own earthly teaching ministry had come to a close, the Father would send His Spirit, the *Spirit of Truth,* to indwell His people and lead them into all truth.

You have a Teacher, Jesus said. *And you have a Father. Therefore, do not expect any man to fill those roles, and don't try to fill them yourselves. Remember, you are all brothers.* (see Matthew 23:9-11)."[18]

FINAL THOUGHTS

Well that is my journey to this point and by the time you read this, I'm sure there will be a need for version 2.
I want to leave you with this thought and a challenge. Seek your purpose for consuming oxygen and occupying space on earth. God put you here for a reason and many of us don't stop to consider it. Regi Campbell produced a workbook *Finding Your Purpose* that will walk you through the process.[1] I established mine and have adjusted it as God has revealed things on my journey. It is very helpful for me to revisit it regularly to keep me on track. It needs to be a fluid document as you journey along.
John Maxwell defined the value of knowing your purpose in his Leadership Bible. "How did Paul's sense of purpose keep him in the battle as he sat in prison? What did he learn behind bars?" Consider the following:

1. A purpose will motivate you.
2. A purpose will keep your priorities straight.
3. A purpose will develop your potential.
4. A purpose will give you power to live in the present.
5. A purpose will help you evaluate your progress.[2]

Understanding your purpose will keep you going through the bad times and the good times as well.

Here is what mine looks like, right now:

> *My purpose is to glorify God by loving and serving others, and by impacting males so that they have an opportunity to make better choices and become the men God designed them to be. Reproducing and multiplying what has been done for me. Helping them grasp the fact that they are valuable to God that while they were still sinners, Christ died for them - showing how much He loves them so they can love and lead others well. Trusting God to produce a movement of men toward Generational Manhood.*

This starts with what every Christian should have as their motivation and purpose, "to glorify God by loving and serving others, and by"…. Then you go from there.

I want to share the sources of what mine has become since my journey began in 2011. "Impacting" comes from *Lifegiving Mentors* by Tim Elmore where he lays out the three levels of leadership. Level one is to "impress" that requires little or no relationship; Level two is to "influence" that requires connection; and Level three is to "impact" that requires both the will of the leader and follower to be involved.[3]

I had previously had "influence" in my statement but after reading this, I want to "impact" people. This can only be done through a mutual relationships and relationship is the only way to make a difference in the lives of others. This book is a valuable resource if you are considering a formal mentoring program because there are forms and processes for establishing an avenue for older people pour into younger ones. It is a gender-neutral approach and helps understand what younger people are looking for and methods they respond best to.

I helped with an addiction rehab program for a season and while I enjoyed the experience, I realized that I was not cut out for the disappointment of the relapse that is almost certain to happen with this group. However, I heard valuable advice during my time there in that success has to be determined by "giving men the opportunity to make a better choice in life." This has served me well and affirmed by Regi Campbell who says that "our role as a mentor is to pour out of our cup into theirs and we are not responsible for filling it nor what they do with it." It is still gut-wrenching to see those you have poured into make decisions that you know will not end well. The Bible says the *a dog will go back to its vomit*. The planting, watering and harvesting principle has to stay in the forefront as you mentor others.

Albert Einstein pointed out the power of compounded interest for wealth. "Multiplication" is much more effective than "addition" in making an impact so my efforts should be focused on those who will do something with what they are given. Reproduction will keep the vision going, otherwise it dies with me. Therefore, my efforts should be focused on sharing what God has taught me with those who will receive it and then multiply it.

A key growth point for me was when I began to grasp the fact that I was valuable to God as His son. This is a sticking point for most of us because we associate our earthly father relationship with our Heavenly Father. Mine was formal and distant though I knew I was loved so that is something I have to battle with constantly. *Fathered by God* is a great resource to work through that process of understanding just how much God loves you.

Jesus kept coming back to this central issue, over and over, driving at it in his teachings, his parables, his penetrating questions. If you look again, through the lens that most of us feel fundamentally fatherless, I think you'll find it very close indeed to the center of Jesus' mission. *Which of you, if his son asks for bread, will give him a stone? Or if he asks for a fish, will give him a snake?* (Matt. 7:9–10 NIV). Well? We rush ahead to the rest of the passage, but I think Jesus is asking us a real question and he wants a real answer. I expect he paused here, his penetrating, compassionate eyes scanning the listeners before him. Well? I hesitate. I guess you're right. I wouldn't, and apart from the exceptionally wicked man, I can't think of any decent father—even if he is self-absorbed—who would do such a thing. Jesus continues, *If you, then, though you are evil, know how to give good gifts to your children, how much more will your Father in heaven give good gifts to those who ask him*! (v. 11 NIV). He is trying to speak to our deepest doubt about the universe.

Look at the birds of the air. Consider the lilies in the field. Are you not much more valuable to your true Father than they? (Matt. 6:26, 28). Hmmm. I'm not sure how to answer. I mean, of course, there's the *right* answer. And then there is the wound in our hearts toward fatherhood, and there is also the way our lives have gone. *What do you think? If a man owns a hundred sheep, and one of them wanders away, will he not leave the ninety-nine on the hills and go to look for the one that wandered off?* (Matt. 18:12 NIV). Yet another question, pressing into the submerged fears in our hearts, another question wanting another answer. Well? Wouldn't he? *And if he finds it, I tell you the truth, he is happier about that one sheep than about the ninety-nine that did not wander off. In the same way your Father in heaven is not willing that any of these little ones should be lost* (vv. 13–14 NIV).

Wherever you are in your ability to believe it at this moment in your life, at least you can see what Jesus is driving at. You have a good Father. He is better than you thought. He cares.

He really does. He's kind and generous. He's out for your best.[4]

Being loved by our Father is what everyone is seeking and finally reaching the point of realizing that He does is key to moving forward in your masculine journey. Dying for my sins is all the proof needed to show it but I have learned to recognize the little things He does for me. I can help others understand the process so they too can learn to be a son.

A man must learn to love and lead well at home before he can be effective in any leadership role. But leading at home is the most important sphere of influence that he has. If it doesn't work at home, don't export it![5] I have come to understand that mentoring efforts should focus on helping men love themselves first in that they see themselves as God does and then love and lead others out of that understanding.

God is not concerned about a program or even a process, He is all about people and relationships. When men are exposed to the love of their Heavenly Father in connection with their brothers, a movement is set in motion. Reproducing and multiplying is not quick or simple. It requires time, emotional investment and sacrifice.

We have two roads that we can travel down in our pursuit of a relationship with God according to *The Cure* by John Lynch, Bruce McNicol and Bill Thrall. There are the roads of "trusting God" or "pleasing God." For so many years I was trying to please God and ended up in "the room of good intentions" where everyone wears a mask because it is an impossible task but I can't let anyone know that I have failed in my self-effort. This recent revelation described what so much of my faith walk has looked like because that is all I knew. I have slowly made my way to the road of trusting God but did not know how to describe it until I read the book. This road leads to "the room of grace" where no perfect people are allowed. The goal there is not that anything gets fixed but that nothing is hidden. We are all saints who sin and having others around who understand and extend grace is so freeing. But I have a tendency to go back trying to please God, thinking He will love me more if I try harder.[7] I am learning that things go better when I just trust God so I am trusting Him to produce the movement and not me!

God is not in a hurry and I am learning to actively wait on Him.

He led the children of Israel in the desert with a cloud by day and a pillar of fire by night that would be over the tabernacle. They would move when God lifted it and camp when it was over the tabernacle. They learned to wait on God and trust His timing. This has been a primary and on-going lesson over my journey. Sometimes I have felt that I was in the wilderness and then God moves and I see the value of waiting. I have realized that sometimes He is preparing me and at times He is preparing others and setting up the right scenario for His purpose to move forward. There is value and purpose for being camped for a period. My efforts are to work on my depth and let Him handle the breadth of my journey.

Sin is generational, and has been well-established over time. However, following God and trying to live His way has been passed on as well. The vision of Generational Manhood has not changed over the years but how to promote and advance the movement has changed dramatically. I am excited to see just how God is going to use me and you to help men understand who they are in Christ and then empower and facilitate their investment of life's experiences and lessons into other men and boys for impact, one life at a time.

"Becoming" is a process that those who have accepted Jesus, have been born again, (John 3:3-8) are supposed to be going through. In *The Cure*, the visual illustration for this process is a butterfly. Though you

> But to all who did receive him, who believed in his name, he gave the right to *become* children of God, who were born, not of blood nor of the will of the flesh nor of the will of man, but of God.
> John 1:12-13 NIV

may see a caterpillar, all of the scientific testing would prove that it is in fact a butterfly. The process is incomplete but it is what it will eventually become.[8] In the same way, I like the analogy of the acorn that in it has everything needed to become a giant oak tree. However, it must be in the right environment, nourished and protected over time to become all that it is designed to be. Just as in physical birth and becoming an adult, there is a process of understanding the way things work. It takes time; it is learned through age-appropriate lessons of success and failure; we need safety and security as we grow; we need someone to show us the way things work to be functional and productive; and we need encouragement and love from others as we grow up. When one or more are not present, there are issues. Spiritual birth and growing up as a child of God require the same elements. Our physical issues can greatly affect our spiritual growth process. Helping men through the mentoring process in recognizing and reconciling both is what God has for me as long as I am on this side. The Bible does not teach that God helps those who help themselves; instead, God helps those who are at the end of themselves. As we come to the end ourselves, we start to become "real." In his devotional post *What Does It Mean To Be Real?*, Steve Arterburn states,

> Being real is the result of being transformed by the love of God. It's not about wealth, or beauty, or power. Heck, most of the time it's suffering, failing, and waiting. Maybe that's why we sometimes miss it. I think the wise old horse in the classic children's story The Velveteen Rabbit says it well. As he explained to the stuffed bunny:
> "It doesn't happen all at once, you become. It takes a long time. That's why it doesn't often happen to people who break easily, or have sharp edges, or who have to be carefully kept. Generally, by the time you are Real, most of your hair has been loved off, and your eyes drop out and you get loose in the joints and very shabby. But these things don't matter at all, because once you are Real you can't be ugly, except to people who don't understand."
> Be real. Open yourself up to God and His transforming power.[9]

I am "becoming" in my walk as His child, becoming "real" and realize there are other brothers I can help but there are also those who need to be adopted into the family – this is my "holy discontent" that has me on the journey. I would love to have you join me.

Now to Him who is able to do immeasurably more than all we ask or imagine, according to His power that is at work within us, to Him be glory in the church and in Christ Jesus throughout all generations, for ever and ever! Amen. Ephesians 3:20-21 NIV

Be on your guard; stand firm in the faith; be courageous; be strong. Do everything in love. 1 Corinthians 16:13-14 NIV

Recognize then Reconcile

So that you can

Love well and Lead well!

BECOME 🌰

NOTES

Introduction
1. Regi Campbell, *What Radical Husbands Do* (Atlanta, Georgia: RM Press, 2014), 2.
2. Tony Dungy, *The Mentor Leader: Secrets to Building People and Teams That Win Consistently* (Carol Stream, Illinois: Tyndale House Publishers, Inc., 2010), 11.
3. Regi Campbell, The Mentoring Manifesto. 1. http://www.radicalmentoring.com (2013).
4. Matthew West. "Do Something." Into the Light, Warner/Chappell Music, Inc., 2012.

Step 1 - Acknowledge the Problem
1. National Fatherhood Initiative. *Father Absence + Involvement Statistics.* http://www.fatherhood.org/father-absence-statistics (September 2018).
2. R. Sanders, *What Was Missing in Sandusky Case? Fathers.* http://www.fatherhood.org (June 29, 2012).
3. John Eldredge, Wild at Heart (Nashville, Tennessee: Thomas Nelson, Inc., 2001), 10.
4. ibid, 83.
5. ibid, 80.
6. ibid, 81.
7. ibid, 53.
8. ibid, 82.
9. ibid, 26.
10. Todd Burpo, *Heaven is for Real: A Little Boy's Astounding Story of His Trip to Heaven and Back* (Thomas Nelson, Kindle Edition, 2010) Kindle Locations 2077-2078.
11. ibid, Kindle Locations 2082-2084.
12. ibid, Kindle Locations 2073-2074.
13. ibid, Kindle Locations 2092-2095.
14. Harold Myra and Marshall Shelley, *The Leadership Secrets of Billy Graham* (Grand Rapids, Michigan: Zondervan, 2005), 197-198
15. Helen H. Lemmel. "Turn Your Eyes Upon Jesus." 1922.
16. Tony Evans, *Kingdom Man* (Carol Streams, Illinois: Tyndale House Publishers, Inc., 2012).
17. Eldredge, 79.
18. John Eldredge. *Fathered by God* (Nashville, Tennessee: Thomas Nelson, Inc., 2009), xi.
19. ibid.
20. ibid, 209.
21. ibid, 213.
22. ibid, 219.

Step 2 - Understand that you have Issues and Decide to Overcome Them
1. John Eldredge, *Wild at Heart* (Nashville, Tennessee: Thomas Nelson, Inc., 2001), 62.
2. ibid, 62.
3. ibid, 65.
4. ibid, 68.
5. ibid, 67.
6. ibid, 71.
7. ibid, 70.
8. ibid, 75.
9. ibid, 91.
10. ibid, 94.
11. Neil S. Wilson, *365 Life Lessons from Bible People* (Carol Stream. Illinois: Tyndale House, 1996).

Step 3 - Seek Forgiveness for Yourself and Then Forgive Others
1. Ingram, Chip and Johnson, Becca. Overcoming Emotions that Destroy: Practical Help for Those Angry Feelings that Ruin Relationships (Grand Rapids, Michigan: Baker Books, 2009), 16.
2. ibid.
3. S. Arturburn, "Grief Not Allowed." March 2004. http://newlife.com
4. Dr. Henry Cloud and Dr. John Townsend, *Boundaries* (Grand Rapids, Michigan: Zondervan, 1992, 2017), 267, 268.
5. Tony Evans, 30 Days to Victory Through Forgiveness (Eugene, Oregon: Harvest House Publishers, 2015).
6. Cloud and Townsend, 257.
7. W. P. Young, "Forgiveness is not about Forgetting it is about Letting Go." https://www.goodreads.com/quotes (February 2018).
8. P. Wilson, "Breathe Grace." http://www.faithgateway.com (March 2018).
9. John Eldredge, *Wild at Heart* (Nashville, Tennessee: Thomas Nelson, Inc, 2001), 107.
10. John Lynch, Radical Mentoring Summit, February 28, 2015.
11. Eldredge, 132.
12. *ibid.*
13. James Bryan Smith, *The Good and Beautiful God* (Downers Grove, Illinois: Inter Varsity Press, 2009), 88.
14. Wes Yoder, *Bond of Brothers* (Grand Rapids, Michigan: Zondervan, 2010), 71.

Step 4 - Understand and Pursue Healthy Relationships
1. Tony Evans, *Kingdom Man* (Carol Streams, Illinois: Tyndale House Publishers, Inc. 2012), 31.
2. John Eldredge, *Wild at Heart* (Nashville, Tennessee: Thomas Nelson, Inc, 2001), 182.
3. ibid. 182.
4. ibid. 184.

5. ibid.
6. ibid. 183.
7. ibid. 187.
8. ibid.
9. D. C. Bissette, "Internet Pornography Statistics: 2003." 2004 http://www.healthymind.com (April 2018)
10. The Call to Biblical Manhood. Man in the Mirror. 6. July, 2004.
11. Tom Buford, "Your Children & Pornography: a guide for Parents." Tommera Press, 2001.
12. Vincent Cyrus Yoder, Thomas B. Virden III, and Kiran Amin. 2005 Internet Pornography and Loneliness: An Association?. *Sexual Addiction & Compulsivity*, Volume 12.1, 2005.
13. Eldredge, 189.
14. Eldredge, 192.
15. Stephen Arterburn, Fred Stoeker, and Mike Yorkey. Every Man's Marriage (Colorado Springs, Colorado: Waterbrook Press, 2003, 2010), 47,49.
16. Eldredge, 193.
17. All Pro Dad. "10 Acts A Chivalrous Husband Does for His Wife." http://www.allprodad.com/10-acts-a-chivalrous-husband-does-for-his-wife (December 2015).
18. Arterburn and Stoeker, and Yorkey, 141.
19. Eldredge, 193.
20. Gary Chapman, The 5 Love Languages (Chicago, Illinois: Northfield Publishing, 1992, 1995, 2004, 2010).
21. Dr. Emerson Eggerichs. "Communicating Love and Respect." http://www.faithgateway.com/communicating-love-respect/ (February 2017).
22. Morgan Snider. "Who Will Carry Your Casket?" http://www.becomegoodsoil.com/who-will-carry-your-casket/ (November 2017).
23. Eldredge, 151.
24. All Pro Dad. "5 Things You Want Said About You at Your Funeral." http://www.allprodad.com/5-things-you-want-said-about-you-at-your-funeral/ (September 2018).

Step 5 - Understand That Evil Exists and Must Be Battled Daily

1. Chip Ingram. "Invisible War, What Every Believer Needs to Know About Satan, Demons & Spiritual Warfare." https://store.livingontheedge.org/product/invisible-war-mp3/ (September 2018).
2. Chip Ingram. "Diabolical, Satan's Agenda for Planet Earth." https://store.livingontheedge.org/product/diabolical-mp3/ (September 2018).
3. John Eldredge. Wild at Heart (Nashville, Tennessee: Thomas Nelson, Inc. 2001), 159 – 170.
4. ibid. 173 – 174.
5. Nate Larkin. Samson and the Pirate Monks (Nashville, Tennessee: Thomas Nelson, Inc. 2006), 57.
6. www.samsonsociety.com
7. Chip Ingram. "Invisible War, What Every Believer Needs to Know

About Satan, Demons & Spiritual Warfare."
https://store.livingontheedge.org/product/invisible-war-mp3/ (September 2018).

Be Somebody and Do Something
1. John C. Maxwell. NIV, The Maxwell Leadership Bible, eBook (Kindle Locations 34392-34394). Thomas Nelson. Kindle Edition.
2. John C. Maxwell. NIV, The Maxwell Leadership Bible, eBook (Kindle Locations 34415-34416). Thomas Nelson. Kindle Edition.
3. Regi Campbell. (2013) The Mentoring Manifesto. 2. www.radicalmentoring.com
4. Radical Mentoring Mentor Summit 2017 – 4/21/2017
5. Henry Blackaby, Richard Blackaby, and Claude King. Experiencing God (Nashville, Tennessee: B&H Publishing Group 2008), 121.
6. ibid. 147, 151.
7. ibid. 161 – 163.
8. Boyd Bailey. "Right Motives." https://www.wisdomhunters.com/right-motives-2/ (July 2016)
9. John C. Maxwell. NIV, The Maxwell Leadership Bible, eBook (Kindle Locations 17809-17811). Thomas Nelson. Kindle Edition.
10. John C. Maxwell. NIV, The Maxwell Leadership Bible, eBook (Kindle Locations 26992-26993). Thomas Nelson. Kindle Edition.
11. John C. Maxwell. NIV, The Maxwell Leadership Bible, eBook (Kindle Locations 73210-73214). Thomas Nelson. Kindle Edition.
12. John C. Maxwell. NIV, The Maxwell Leadership Bible, eBook (Kindle Locations 22777-22793). Thomas Nelson. Kindle Edition.
13. Tim Elmore. Lifegiving Mentors, A Guide for Investing Your Life in Others (Norcross, Georgia: Growing Leaders, Inc. 2008, 2009), 112.
14. ibid.110.
15. John Eldredge. Fathered by God (Nashville, Tennessee: Thomas Nelson, Inc, 2009), 8 – 11.
16. Steve Corbett and Brian Fikkert. When Helping Hurts: how to alleviate poverty without hurting the poor – and yourself (Chicago, Illinois: Moody Publishers, 2009, 2012), 55.
17. ibid. 207-208.
18. Nate Larkin. Samson and the Pirate Monks (Nashville, Tennessee: Thomas Nelson, Inc. 2006), 102-103.

Final Thoughts
1. Regi Campbell. "Finding Your Purpose." https://radicalmentoring.com/wp-content/uploads/2013/05/Finding-Your-Purpose.pdf (September 2013).
2. John C. Maxwell. NIV, The Maxwell Leadership Bible, eBook (Kindle Locations 88152-88157). Thomas Nelson. Kindle Edition.
3. Tim Elmore. Lifegiving Mentors, A Guide for Investing Your Life in Others (Norcross, Georgia: Growing Leaders, Inc. 2008, 2009), 15.
4. John Eldredge. Fathered by God (Nashville, Tennessee: Thomas Nelson, Inc, 2009), 29 – 31.
5. John C. Maxwell. NIV, The Maxwell Leadership Bible, eBook (Kindle

Locations 20171-20179). Thomas Nelson. Kindle Edition.
    6. Albert Mohler. "Fighting the Enemy Through Prayer." http://www.faithgateway.com/fighting-enemy-prayer/#.WmOlEZM-eu4 (January 2018)
    7. John Lynch, Bruce McNicol, and Bill Thrall. The Cure (Phoenix, Arizona: Trueface, 2011), 12-23.
    8. ibid.49.
    9. NewLife. "What Does It Mean to Be Real?" https://newlife.com/real/ (January 2018).

THE AUTHOR

Tim is a dedicated husband to his wife Jill
and a father to their adult children Abby, Olivia, and Chandler.
Tim and Jill live in Fair Play, South Carolina.
Challenged to be the one to *Do Something* about the problem of
a shortage of male mentors, Tim has been on a journey of
discovering more about the problem,
the solution, and himself in the process.
Fatherlessness is the problem but the solution to it quite complex in
that men have to understand their issues and then be willing to deal
with them before being able to help other men. Healing takes time
but it has to start with recognition then reconciliation of the
wounds received during childhood that manifest in adults.
We do have a problem that
somebody needs to do something about!
Join in the pursuit of generational manhood
by ReBuilding Real Men.

Made in the USA
Las Vegas, NV
02 February 2022